Alfred Joshua Butler

Court Life in Egypt

Alfred Joshua Butler

Court Life in Egypt

ISBN/EAN: 9783743310087

Manufactured in Europe, USA, Canada, Australia, Japa

Cover: Foto ©Thomas Meinert / pixelio.de

Manufactured and distributed by brebook publishing software (www.brebook.com)

Alfred Joshua Butler

Court Life in Egypt

AN EGYPTIAN VILLAGE IN FLOOD-TIME.

BY

ALFRED J. BUTLER,

FELLOW OF BRASENOSE COLLEGE, OXFORD,

AUTHOR OF "THE ANCIENT COPTIC CHURCHES OF EGYPT."

WITH ILLUSTRATIONS.

LONDON: CHAPMAN AND HALL
LIMITED
1887

CONTENTS.

CHAPTER I.

A volcano by night—The Under-Governor of Alexandria—Reception by the Khédive—Departure for Upper Egypt—Travelling companions—A Beduin sham-fight—Scenes at Siût—Dancing-girls at Girgah—The Cataract and Philae—Advantages of consular protection—Ducal enterprise . . 1

CHAPTER II.

Dining with the Khedive—Horrors of the Dôsah—Visit to Maidûm—Adventure with Beduins—Mirage—Ball at 'Abdîn Palace—Story of the murdered Mufettish—Naib's extravagance—Palace quarters 34

CHAPTER III.

Journey in Lower Egypt—Sulimân—Dinner with 'Abdu 'l 'Al—Ruins at Thmuis—Damietta—Zagazig—Miseries of Tantah—The sirocco—Encounter with a lunatic—Rosetta—Smelling the zephyr 65

CHAPTER IV.

Mr. Gladstone and Turkey—An unjust steward—The devil's muezzin—Colonel Gordon and the Khedive—First signs of the Rebellion—Stories of fortunes—The pyramids in summer—Great procession of dervishes 93

CHAPTER V.

Alexandria—Palace by the sea—Oriental luxury—The *valet-de-chambre*—A sail—Narrow escape of the Khedive—Fête in the palace gardens—Morice Bey—The sea-shore—Picnic in the desert 121

CHAPTER VI.

Conversations with the Khedive—Slave trade—Egyptian morals—The Dôsah—The month of fasting—Ceremony at the palace—Superstitious customs—Ramleh sportsmen—Story of the Sultan—" Our own correspondent "—Story of Fakri Pasha—An unpleasant journey 149

CHAPTER VII.

Summer and Winter—Riaz Pasha—The Dôsah again—Slavery and England—The splendour of the Mufettish—Colonel Gordon—Bribing *The Times*—The Khedive and his father—Ismail and Russia 187

CONTENTS.

CHAPTER VIII.

The pyramids in flood-time—Beset by Beduins—Ancient coins—Pistols forgotten—Stories of Arab "saints"—The Mahmal—**Festival** of Great Bairam—The Chief Eunuch—Visit to Sheikh Mohammed es Sadât—The King's chamber . . 210

CHAPTER IX.

Black arts — **Khedive and** magician — A Coptic dealer in charms—Remarkable Persian ceremony—Sanguinary rites—Litany and lections—More talk about the Dôsah—Arab myths 238

CHAPTER X.

Wild flowers at Ramleh—The Dôsah to be abolished—The Khedive's intentions about the slave-trade—Difficulties **and** opposition—Daûd Pasha **and the** brigands—Treasure-trove—The golden lions—Turkish comedy—A princess's wedding . 261

CHAPTER XI.

Mutiny of the three colonels—Decision of the cabinet council—Conversation with the Khedive—Making an earthquake—Visit of **a** Persian **grandee—His** reflections on Egypt—The Prophet's birthday—The Dôsah actually abolished—Conclusion 283

LIST OF ILLUSTRATIONS.

Bas-relief of Seti I. at Abydos	To face p.	21
Painted Statues of Rahotep and Nefert (Bulak Museum)	,,	46
Mushrabîah Window in Cairo	,,	61
Ancient House at Rosetta	,,	89
An Egyptian Village in Flood-time	,,	171
Group of Beduins	,,	211
Persian Brass-worker	,,	254
Native Mimes and Minstrels	,,	280

COURT LIFE IN EGYPT.

CHAPTER I.

A volcano by night—The Under-Governor of Alexandria—Reception by the Khedive—Departure for Upper Egypt—Travelling companions—A Beduin sham-fight—Scenes at Siût—Dancing-girls at Girgah—The Cataract and Philae—Advantages of consular protection—Ducal enterprise.

It was in January, 1880, that I received a telegram summoning me out to Egypt as tutor to the sons of the Khedive; and, though a friend long familiar with the East pledged his knowledge of orientals that the order meant no hurry for a month or two, I judged it better to obey more literally. As yet I had not learned the Egyptian proverb, "Haste is of the devil."

So I was soon on board a French packet sailing away from the Bay of Naples, not sorry to have so bright a scene for the last clear view in Europe. As we stood out to sea, we beheld the red palace on the shore where the ex-Khedive Ismail was living in discontented splendour. Just then, too, he was in a state of livid indignation, for one of his slave-girls had dared to escape and fly with a handsome Neapolitan officer. In Egypt the slave would have been recaptured and killed: in Italy, where Ismail's arm was shortened, she married, and doubtless lived and lives in happy security. To be set at defiance by a civilised elopement must have bitten like acid into Ismail's spirit; no wonder that he forthwith sent his son, Prince Hassan, to Constantinople, begging the Sultan's leave to reside at Stambûl, where the swift and sharp methods of oriental revenge still flourish. I shall have a good deal to say hereafter about Ismail Pasha, that curious figure, half Harûn er Rashîd and half Pharaoh, on the stage of the nineteenth century.

At night we sailed calmly on through phosphorescent seas, and before dawn I was called to see the island cone of Stromboli which shot forth fountains of flame at intervals, like the fitful light of some giant's forge. Sometimes only a faint glow broke through the gloom: sometimes a column of spreading fire towered above the crater; strange starlike gleams flashed out upon the dark sides of the mountain; or floods of lava thundered down in burning cataracts. Then all again was still, and the volcano was shrouded in silence and darkness. As we passed Messina, a rising storm obscured the distant lights of the town: the coast vanished: and for three days we tossed in rain and gloom. Then almost on a sudden we came into a new world of sunshine, and found the ship gliding through golden air and still waters into the harbour of Alexandria.

Soon after we had cast anchor a fleet of little boats beset our vessel. I waited on board ship till an Egyptian officer in naval uniform stepped up to me, and with a salute inquired my name in English. On ascertaining it, he introduced to me his companion as the Under-Governor of Alexandria. With great ceremony they conducted me to a splendid ten-oared galley, where I reclined on cushions of crimson velvet and gold, and was rowed ashore to the Arsenal. There the officer took his leave, the crew saluted, and the Under-Governor led me to a carriage which was waiting. We passed through the streets of Alexandria under countless salutes and salâms. My companion pointed out this and that building and asked my opinion of the town, but after every remark pointed to his own heart, and added, laughing softly,

"Et moi, je suis le Sous-Gouverneur d'Alexandrie." I displayed as much enthusiasm for the second-rate edifices as my conscience would carry, inly contrasting them with the famous temples and palaces of Alexander's city, and I congratulated my friend on his exalted dignity. Our progress ended at the Court tailor's, where I was measured for my destined uniform. Thence to the Hôtel d'Europe in the Place Méhémet 'Ali, beneath the windows of which some two and a half years later the worst scenes of 'Arâbi's massacre were enacted. With one more assurance of his rank the Under-Governor left me till the morning.

At seven o'clock next day the faithful magnate was in waiting. His merry eye twinkled and his voice gurgled with a prolonged chuckle over his own good fortune and mine, as he took me again to the tailor and thence to the station. He gave me a letter to Zeki Pasha, Grand Master of the Ceremonies to the Khedive, and I thanked him for all his kindness. "Mais non, monsieur : vous n'avez que Son Altesse à remercier, dont je suis le très humble serviteur. Ah! mon Dieu, monsieur, quelle chance que la vôtre : vous serez à la Cour, auprès des petits princes, près de Son Altesse. Et moi je suis le Sous-

Governeur d'Alexandrie!" It was a hard struggle to keep grave, but I saw his drift and told him I would report the kind treatment I had received to the Khedive. Upon this his face beamed again: again he shook hands, and there blent with the screech of the engine-whistle, as the train moved off, soft murmurs of " d'Alexandrie."

At Cairo a Court official was waiting to receive me, and conducted me to the New Hotel, a showy building erected by Ismail Pasha to accommodate his guests at the opening of the Suez Canal. Shortly after my arrival Turâbi Bey, English Secretary to the Khedive, called on behalf of His Highness to bid me welcome and to say that I should be received at Court in a day or two. He spoke very highly of the Khedive's kindness. Next day he called again with a message of inquiry from His Highness, and brought the good news that the Khedive would start in a week's time for a tour in Upper Egypt. He also introduced me to a very beautiful young Jewess of Alexandria, who, though only sixteen years old, talked English almost perfectly, besides German, French, Italian, and a little Arabic. But polyglot children are common enough in Egypt.

When Turâbi left I called on Rogers Bey, then

the greatest living Arabic scholar among Englishmen*
not excepting even Professor Palmer. The natives
always said that he was the only foreigner who could
talk not merely as one of themselves but better than
the best of them. He told me that the Arabs all
believed that the Khedive was going into Upper
Egypt for the purpose of unearthing and bringing
home a vast treasure of jewels and gold of which
tidings had reached him. How else, they argued,
would a man in his position undertake such a troublesome journey? Clearly impossible.

On the day appointed for my reception by the
Khedive I drove to 'Abdin Palace, where he always
spends the daytime. I was shown into an ante-room,
where aides-de-camp, officers of the ceremonies, and
other officials were lounging about and smoking.
When summoned to the presence, I passed through
other ante-rooms gorgeously furnished, up a fine
marble staircase, and into a large saloon, where the
Khedive was sitting alone. He rose as I entered,
shook hands, and motioned me to a seat beside him.
I of course was dressed in my new uniform, and
wore the red tarbûsh or fez, which may never be
removed. To uncover in presence of the sovereign

* Rogers Bey died in 1884.

would be gross impertinence. It is hard to say a good word for the fez, which is simply the turban stripped of its outer bandage, *i e.*, of all that made it beautiful to the eye, and effectual as a protection from the sun. The uniform otherwise is really European, a sort of frock-coat with stiff collar: in fact, when the pashas decided to abandon their flowing robes, they sought Europe through for a model of respectability in costume, and fixed on the dress of the British parson. Artistically, it makes a sad show beside the bright and graceful raiment of the East: physically, it is the most uncomfortable and unsuitable garment possible in a hot climate: but these drawbacks are meant to be forgotten in its moral significance. Perhaps rather the Turk has refined on the proverb with true oriental subtilty; and the wolf is dressed in shepherd's clothing.

On entering the presence one has to button up the frock-coat, or stambouline as it is called, just as the natives cover up their hands in their long sleeves. But nothing could be less formal or more pleasant than the Khedive's manner. A frank smiling face, a winning voice, and a dignified quiet demeanour, invest his person with a charm which he has inherited from his father, and has bequeathed to his children.

He talked affably while I smoked the proffered cigarette : for singularly enough the Khedive is the only oriental I ever met who never smokes. I took the opportunity of telling the native story about the buried treasure. The Viceroy laughed, but answered with evident sincerity that the only treasure he desired was the prosperity and contentment of his people.

Before the interview was over, he gave me to understand that he was very pleased with me, that he felt sure the young princes would be pleased likewise, and that he hoped to improve his English by conversing with me often. To which I replied that I should deem it an honour to be of service to His Highness, and withdrew, making the customary salâm.

The three or four days which remained before our departure for Upper Egypt, I naturally spent in seeing the streets and mosques of Cairo,—sights which every traveller is familiar with, and most have written books upon. It is not my purpose to describe here scenes of the kind : though no one could delight more in the brightness and picturesqueness of the Victorious City,* in the romance of its life, and the wealth of its art.

* Cairo, *i.e.* Masr el Kahirah, means, of course, Masr the Victorious.

On the eve of our departure I drove with Turâbi Bey to our steamer to examine our quarters. Turâbi, though a Turk by birth, had lived many years in England attached to the Turkish Embassy, and was a loyal Englishman at heart. I was pleased to share his cabin. But when we went below we were horrified to find nothing but a bare mattrass in each berth, with no sign of blankets or linen. With the natives these are superfluous luxuries; and the steamer for the suite was unluckily at the mercy of a native. Next morning, therefore, besides our regular luggage, we had to take linen, towels, and even soap. I soon began to find that even among eastern princes all is not magnificence. The fact was that the Khedive had given orders for the comfort of the few Europeans with him: but his native servants interpreted these orders in native fashion. Indeed, the Marshal of the Palace was an enfranchised slave, who joined utter ignorance of European ways to a fanatic hatred of all Franks; a hatred veiled at times under cold and steely smiles, but more often scowling in every line of his most repulsive countenance. I learnt in time how to deal with him, and, when need arose, crossed swords with him unflinchingly.

It was on the 22nd of January, 1880, that we

started on our voyage. Nearly the whole Court went, and the party required three large steamers besides a provision-boat. By request of the Khedive, I kept a journal, but shall record here a good deal of personal matter there omitted, and omit most of the descriptions and events there recorded. Every one knows the glow of Egyptian sunlights and sunsets, the majestic sameness of the Nile, the sublimities of Karnak and Philae; not every one has traversed the land and visited the monuments of the Pharaohs in the company of the living "king of Egypt."

Our meals on this expedition were at first very trying. For breakfast one had nothing but a piece of bread with two kinds of condiment, rose-leaf jam and olives, in two little saucers. Olives in oil are specially difficult to relish at seven o'clock in the morning. We lunched at noon, and dined at seven, *i.e.* whenever the provision-boat happened to be within reach: but she was a slow craft, and generally overtook us, as an Arab would say, at the time appointed by destiny.

Luncheon and dinner were much alike, and I may quote a specimen. The five Europeans and Turâbi sat together at a round table formed by a large tray: each had a plate and a knife and a fork. The first course consisted of turkey or chicken cut into lumps; next bamias, or Egyptian beans, swimming in oil; thirdly a whole sheep; then dolmas, or rice wrapped in cabbage-leaves; then mutton bones; then pilâf, a preparation of rice; then a sugared pasty; and lastly oranges and bananas. For side-dishes we had lettuce drenched with oil, raw turnips sliced and soaked in oil, and a creamy-looking compound of garlic, said to be very delicious by people who have cultivated the taste. I, for one, could never make the *premier pas qui coûte.*

After every meal servants were in attendance with napkins, ewers, and basins. One servant holds the basin, while another pours a stream of fresh water over the hands. Some of the natives, while performing their ablutions, made a thick lather of soap, which they thrust into their mouths, using a finger as a toothbrush. Another trick they have even less delectable, that of making eructations to denote and to ease repletion. To do this is regarded as a proof of politeness: it is like saying to your host, "What a splendid dinner we have eaten." Men remarkable for polish and breeding make the noise in their host's face on taking leave, and I have heard the good man in answer murmur his gratified " God reward you." There is a "candy deal of courtesy" in eastern manners.

The soldiers of our escort squatted in circles of five or six round a single dish, into which they plunged their fingers emulously and ravenously.

I may here introduce some of my companions. Turâbi Bey I have already mentioned, a jovial sturdy little Turk of sixty years, with a kindly pleasant face and a loyal heart, with the tottering gait of a child and the appetite of a giant, never happy without a cigarette, yet the model of misery when forced for politeness' sake to smoke a cigar; a first-rate English scholar, yet incapable of uttering one sentence in the native Arabic after fifteen years residence in Egypt, always grumbling yet never ill-tempered, to me the cheeriest of companions and best of friends, to the Khedive most devoted of servants and often wisest of counsellors. Poor Turâbi! Just four years after the time of which I am writing I witnessed the pomp of his funeral, and stood beside his grave outside the walls of Cairo, as his body was lowered in its Muslim shroud and the 'Ulema chanted their prayers above his last resting-place. I never recall that day without sorrow, nor his memory without affection.

The Europeans in the suite of the Khedive were four besides myself. Goudard Bey, for many years Chef du Cabinet to Ismail and occupying the same position with Tewfik, the reigning Khedive. He was a Frenchman of some fifty years, astute, scholarly, parsimonious, speaking no language but his own; an oval face with pointed beard, a high voice, occasional dry laughless humour, and a reserve of manner which aimed at silence afloat and at invisibility ashore. Tonino Bey, Master of Ceremonies, an Italian born in Egypt, spoke French and Arabic, told and still tells most moving and romantic stories, in which he figures as hero, and princesses of various countries serve as heroines; cracks jokes, knows everybody, is quite adapted to the most native of native ways, *vultu mutabilis, albus et ater.* Martino Bey, who has now succeeded Goudard, is a fine handsome Italian, well-dressed and well-mannered, fluent in French, fair at Arabic, a good *raconteur*, cynical and contemptuous of his surroundings, but wise as a weasel among them. Lastly came a pleasant and rollicking young Austrian soldier, quick-tempered and known to have killed an adversary in duel with a sword-thrust a few months ago, otherwise perfect in manner, master of six languages, a soldier of fortune who had seen service from Abyssinia to Mexico.

We were therefore a motley company to be travelling together, to say nothing of the fact that the *entourage* of the Khedive included Turks, Circassians, Sudanese, and an Armenian, as well as Egyptians. But we got on very well: and in the Babel of tongues one had never far to seek for an interpreter. Cards and chess beguiled the evening hours, and I soon learned that "check" is merely the Arabic "sheikh," that "checkmate" is "esh sheikh mât," or "the chief is dead," and that "rook" means "rukn" or corner-piece. Among the more general lessons which I got by heart, the golden rule was *nil admirari:* so if I saw a bey devour five feet of sugar-cane in as many seconds, or a pasha cleaning his boots with his handkerchief, I never betrayed astonishment or even curiosity. Another great secret in dealing with orientals is to put a good face on everything. A third maxim is, be ready to give all the information you possess: what may seem childish to you, will be novel to them. The man after their own heart is "renowned for the shining calm of manners, the morning light of knowledge, and the smiling of the mouth."

Some of their manners and customs are very curious. For instance, I could not help occasionally witnessing the toilette of a certain bey. His first operation, before proceeding to wash, was to swathe his body round and round in bands of flannel up to the very throat. Having thus guarded himself against the contact of the water, he gently dabbed his cheeks and hands, dried himself, and was clean. For his hair he had a pair of brushes, which he used as follows: filling his mouth as full as it would hold with water, he spirted it all out suddenly on the brushes, and then whisked and whirled them about his head. The hair, of course, is worn so short that no further arrangement is necessary. This was bad enough; but it is only among the lower orders that one sees how very dirty the natives are in their very cleanliness. The mosque tanks are filled with water, which is replenished but never changed; in the slime of these green and fetid pools I have seen men wash first their feet, then face and hands, and lastly rinse out their mouths.

All along our route on either side of the river the fellahín thronged out of their villages with banners flying and tom-toms beating. At Wasta, our first station, some Beduins formed a course beside our vessels and entertained us with a display of their horsemanship, manœuvring in mock battle, pointing and firing their flint-locks in the midst of wild charges. Scimetars, pistols, and spears gleamed through a storm of dust; wild war-cries rose above the thunder of hoofs. When the combat was over, and the weary warriors had gone to cut sugar-cane for their dinner, their place was taken by crowds of poor people, who sat in long lines before the Khedive's steamer, thinking hours of patient watching well rewarded by a glimpse of their sovereign.

At Beni Suif the Khedive drove in state to the mosque, like a good Musulman. Thence we passed to Miniah, and anchored at sundown before the palace. Its walls, which align the shore for half a mile, were flashing from end to end with lights; and in front long rows of lamps and portfires shone, making a scene of real splendour. The Khedive at once drove through the town. All the streets were adorned on either side with continuous arches of painted woodwork, and every arch was hung with flags and lanterns. Here and there, perched in boxes over the roadway in mid-air, groups of musicians or storytellers recited or sang, to the great amusement of the crowd below. Sometimes, beneath one of these boxes, we had to fight our way, shoulder to shoulder, through a dense mob; but they took it all with great good humour. The scene was entirely oriental; the narrow streets decked with costly hangings and lanterns; the bazaars or frontless shops with floors raised two feet above the ground, and grave, bearded merchants sitting cross-legged on Persian carpets; robes, turbans, and faces of every hue and type, an ever-changing kaleidoscope of bright colours. Whenever we reached the house of a notable or rich merchant, a band of music struck up a salute, slaves salâmed, and carpets were spread for us to walk upon across the courtyard. Within the house we entered first a marble hall, then a saloon called the guest-room, where our host greeted us, and where coffee, syrup, and cigarettes were served; while native minstrels performed on strange instruments or sang Arabian ditties.

At Manfalût I saw for the first time the religious ceremony called the "zikr," a sort of dramatic prayer, in this case for the welfare of the Khedive. Two rows of turbaned dervishes stood facing each other; while they sang their feet never moved, but, as the music rose or fell, their bodies swayed from side to side or bowed lowly forward, till the turbans of the two ranks nearly touched. Arab music generally strikes one as a dull hubbub, but in this chant there was something pathetic and pleasing. The "zikr" is much used at all great religious festivals.

We reached Siût, or Assiût, the capital of Upper Egypt, on January 28th. There thousands of people stood on the banks, and cannon thundered in salute as the Khedive touched land in the early afternoon. The hottest part of the day once past, towards four o'clock His Highness started in a state carriage for the town. The procession was headed by some native horsemen; then came a standard-bearer with green turban denoting his descent from the Prophet; bare-legged runners or saises in white tunics and vests splendidly broidered in colours and gold; next part of the mounted guard; then the Khedive drawn by a pair of black horses. Ten more guardsmen followed, and after them the suite, mounted as best they could, *i. e.* on donkeys. Close behind and on either side thronged Beduins on their prancing Arabs, and then the population.

The road of course was only a raised causeway of ordinary Nile mud, and lay three inches deep in dust. The effect may be imagined when a vast mob, horse and foot, were rushing on together all with the one idea of keeping as close to the Khedive as possible. Fortunately I had secured a very good donkey, and a donkey-boy, who fought tooth and nail and managed by some means to keep me in my place just behind the guardsmen all the afternoon. For a mile, through air literally darkened with dust, we pushed on to the city. The narrow gateway barely allowed room for His Highness's carriage to pass; and when the guardsmen were through, and the crowd came all storming the one point, the usual result followed. For a moment we were all wedged immoveably together; then, being well in the centre of the archway, I saw the foremost on either side fall heavily and disappear under a heap of fresh bodies flung over them by pressure from behind. I thought bones must have been broken, if not lives lost, but in the East such accidents are not reported. As the sides yielded, the centre was relieved; and my donkey, after a desperate struggle to avoid being swept off his feet, brought me through the press in triumph. In the town the Khedive was greeted with music and shouts from the soldiers. The men as a rule make a great deal of obeisance, but are silent: they do not know how to cheer: but the women on the housetops raise their shrill "ul-ul-ul" (doubtless the Latin *ululatus*) which is used to express either joy or mourning.

As we wound through the narrow streets, the scene was indescribably vivid and amusing. In front of the procession all was calm and quiet, behind a confused battle for place was incessantly raging. A staff of beaters came to the rescue of the suite, and with long sticks belaboured the crowd till they reversed the pressure. Even the donkey-boy would lay his cudgel smartly across the shoulders of a man twice his size. A hundred blows were falling on every side; none were resented or returned. Of course there was also a ceaseless by-play made up of little incidents. Now a luckless Arab lost his shoe in the mêlée and followed plunging, diving, and swearing, as it was kicked about by all comers; another was seen wildly smiting the head of his neighbours with an ivory fiddlestick, without damage on either side; there again a scimetar or battle-axe swings round and makes a momentary way for its owner; there a huge burly officer rolls ignominiously off his donkey amid shouts of laughter; later on a man rushes to the Khedive's carriage with a censer of burning incense, and the odour is sweet in one's

CALIFORNIA

BAS-RELIEF OF SETI I. AT ABYDOS.

still. But I brought him to the shore at last, and dismounted,—rather proud of having reserved the act for the end of the journey.

Another Ptolemaic temple awaited us at Esnah, but there was nothing else to detain us there: and next day we started on our last stage to the Cataract. It was long past sundown when the lights of Assuân were seen in the distance. For the last three miles the navigation was slow and dangerous: indeed, had not the townsfolk marked out our course by placing lanterns on the rocky islets and light-ships on the shoals, we should not have reached our destination that night. Towards eight o'clock, however, our steamers were anchored fast, and those who were wise among us ran ashore to make their purchases of ostrich-feathers, ivory, silver ornaments, or savage weapons from the Sudân, knowing well that to-morrow all prices would be trebled in the Khedive's honour.

Next morning, as I was leisurely dressing, there came a sudden order,—"His Highness is starting." In three minutes I was on deck, and found the Khedive and suite embarking in four large eight-oar galleys. It was not eight o'clock, but already the sun was burning fiercely, boding ill to a traveller unfortified by a morsel of breakfast. But there was no help for it: the view of the Cataract was in question. First we were rowed across to Elephantine Island, where the ancient Nilometer was visited and other ruins; thence steadily up stream amid scenery that became at every stroke more and more interesting. On the right was a line of rocky hills covered for the most part with a shroud of golden sand—sand of a ruddy golden hue, with a far richer and deeper glow than the pale yellow of the sea-shore or the desert: on the left, from grey flats upon the water's edge, jagged and broken crags rose sloping away to the mountains beyond. The mountain-tops were generally crowned with tombs or ruins, and often on the face of a waterworn boulder one noticed some ancient hieroglyphic.

Crowds of Arabs followed us along the shore, and astonished us by their skill in climbing up and down precipices, where there seemed no footing even for a cat. As we advanced, the gorge narrowed, till at last the force of the current, shut in between great walls of rock, became too strong for rowing. Then, after a journey of two hours, we landed and climbed over hills strewn with all sorts of beautiful stones, granite, quartz, syenite, &c., which last, of course, is so called from Syene, the old Greek name of Assuân. As we reached at last a lofty eminence, a view of the river opened quite unlike any view of the Nile we had seen. The water was spread out into a vast lake sown thick with small rocky islands on which palm-trees were waving; between these isles the stream was flowing in hundreds of still, azure channels, or foaming in fierce rapids among boulders that blocked the way, and a continuous roar of thunder filled our ears. Round the great basin cliffs and hills stood clear in dazzling sunshine, and above it the skies shone like a dome of sapphire.

On our way back Turâbi Bey, who, like me, had eaten no breakfast, managed to get a small crust of bread from a native. Like the good soul he was he offered me a share, which of course I declined, and it was near midday when we reached our steamers, sick and faint but thankful to have escaped a sun-stroke.

But the day's work was not half over: we had yet to see Philae, the island above the Cataract. There is a short line of railway for conveying goods round the falls, and by this we were to travel. A picturesque ride among palms and sunflowers and across a stretch of sand brought us to the station, where a luggage-train alone was visible. This, however, was our special. Four trucks, decked with palm-branches and set with chairs, served for the Court. The Khedive and a favoured few, among whom I counted, rode in the guard's van, which was covered with flags and flowers outside and hung with silks and mirrors within. Half-an-hour's jolting through the desert brought us opposite Philae, where a steamer was waiting to take us across to the island, which lies opposite to the gate of the Cataract. The scenery around is wild, wonderful, enchanting; the very ruins seem now to have become part of nature, as they stand in magnificent repose, the centre of a scene for romantic beauty and historic interest unequalled in the world. One can never forget that last view of Philae—ruin, rock, and river, all touched with the gorgeous colours of an Egyptian sunset.

In the evening the Khedive remained on board his steamer, his band playing various music; some English airs were kindly ordered on behalf of the only Englishman present. Coffee was served from a golden vessel in cups of gold studded with diamonds, and silver lamps were burning near; on shore countless lanterns were swinging among the palm-trees. Oddly enough, when the English national anthem was played, it was accompanied by a loud salute of cannon. I little thought then how soon thousands of English troops would be hurrying past that very spot to victories of barren splendour and fruitless death in the Sudân. But the strain was again interrupted, as a powerful native band struck up within a stone's-throw of the steamer. The discord was enough to tear nerves of iron, but it was well-meant and borne by the Khedive with great good-humour. And even when a solitary Arab came down to the water's edge and beat with loyal fury his tom-tom, tin-kettle, or other execrable instrument, he was allowed to din away unmolested.

On the 5th February our bows pointed northward again, and Assûan soon faded away behind us, not without sharp regret. Juvenal might have had a far worse place of banishment. At Edfû we saw the famous temple, and were escorted back by a troop of Beduin mounted on camels. All the way they kept up a mimic battle, and the beasts charged and wheeled with a nimble swiftness that upset all one's ideas taken from the sedate and awkward gait of the laden camel. I need not chronicle our visit to Luxor and Karnak, to "hundred-gated Thebes," and the Valley of the Tombs of the Kings. All travellers know them: no writer can do them justice.

Our three days at Luxor we lived mostly at the hotel, and were not sorry for the change of diet. The English Consul here, named Mustafa 'Agha, entertained us kindly; his son not only talked English well but had a real knowledge of ancient Egyptian history. I shall long remember, however, his good services to me. In the matter of antiques I was at this time a very ignorant novice, and young Mustafa offered to make my purchases. He took me to a dealer; I fancied a couple of figures and asked the price. "Eighty francs," said the Arab. In the course of half-an-hour's altercation my guide beat him down to fifty francs, announcing every fall with a look of triumph and telling me not to give way. Then came a furious contest; the dealer would not yield another franc, and Mustafa swore he would not give a piastre more than forty francs. They yelled and foamed in each other's faces, their eyes flashed, they clutched and tore at each other's raiment. When they seemed at the point of a death-struggle, Mustafa made a sudden dash at the figures, seized them, and flew downstairs, shouting to me "Give him forty francs!" I gave the money, which the dealer received in sulky submission, and, following downstairs, I overtook Mustafa. That worthy handed me the figures, one of which he had broken in three pieces meanwhile by letting it fall, but he assured me that I had got a glorious bargain, and that the breakage rather enhanced the value. At this my crude suspicions were fully aroused, but too late: I was fairly caught. The figures were worth eight or ten francs at the outside, and I have no doubt that Mustafa scored a napoleon as his share of the transaction. This was my first experience of bakshîsh in the Egyptian system of commerce.

Before we left, however, I paid another visit to the dealer alone; and, being now unprotected by Her Britannic Majesty's consul, I fared much better: for I bought for a small sum some really curious and rare antiques, which I still treasure. When I showed them to Mustafa, he could not conceal his chagrin, but remarked, "Ah, I told you that he would take in the end whatever you offered."

I confess I was not sorry to hear a few weeks later that Mustafa had been paid in his own coin. One of the many Rothschilds was travelling in Egypt that winter, and was announced to visit Luxor. Good Mustafa 'Agha made immense preparations for the event,—horses and donkeys, guards, Beduins, illuminations, fireworks. The great man arrived, and a three days' festival was held in his honour: even the Khedive had hardly a more magnificent reception. Everybody knew when the affair was over that a tremendous bakshish had been earned. Fellah said to fellah, "O my brother, this was the Lord Treasurer of the English, and all the mines of India are in his hand. Wallâhi, why was not I born Mustafa 'Agha?" And in due time a heavy box came from Cairo,—so heavy that Mustafa feared it could contain only silver plate, and he was hoping for costly jewels. It proved to contain—two dozen of champagne. This for a Musulman, who may not drink wine, was cruel indeed. Yet in time Mustafa recovered the blow, and talked of sending a ham to the donor.

Our few remaining days on the Nile passed pleasantly enough. When actually travelling one had always a pasha to play chess with or smoke with on deck; sunshine to bask in and coffee to sip; a treasured copy of Homer to read or a dialogue in Turkish or Arabic to watch, rather than hear, and despair of ever understanding. In the evening we had music and fireworks, and sometimes a round game of cards with the Khedive, in which case we always played with counters, never for money. At Siût the Khedive received a telegram from the Duke of Sutherland, then in Cairo, begging for a speedy interview. The duke, ever dauntless in enterprise, had been trying to negociate for the purchase or for the lease of the Egyptian railways, and, being on the point of leaving for England, wished to have a decisive answer on the subject. The Khedive reached Cairo only to find the duke departed. Subsequently the duke's agent, Mr. Easton, asked me whether we had not made a very slow passage from Siût—whether in fact our arrival had not been purposely retarded. I replied that our rate of speed had varied all the journey through, and that I had ceased to notice it— an answer which closed the conversation. But the duke's scheme came to nothing.

CHAPTER II.

Dining with the Khedive—Horrors of the Dôsah—Visit to Maidûm—Adventure with Beduins—Mirage—Ball at 'Abdin Palace—Story of the murdered Mufettish—Naib's extravagance—Palace quarters.

ONCE again in Cairo, I returned to the hotel with nothing to do. "The rooms in the palace are not ready yet," was the invariable answer to any inquiries I made about beginning work; and I soon ceased to trouble my head on the matter. It was very pleasant to wander about the mosques and bazaars, to ride in the desert, to visit ancient tombs and pyramids, or to have a day's quiet shooting among the rich clover and corn across the Nile; while for duty I had to lounge away a few hours in the palace anterooms occasionally. In this manner I picked up a little Arabic and some acquaintance with native habits and modes of thought.

The Khedive lives with his wife and family at the palace of Ismalia, near the Nile bridge. He is a strict monogamist, loyal in his married life as any European, and detests slavery as much as polygamy; all his attendants are paid servants. He rises at four or five o'clock every morning, eats no breakfast, but takes two hours' exercise, walking or driving, and between seven and eight o'clock drives in state to 'Abdin palace, which is about half a mile distant from Ismailia. 'Abdin is the usual place of reception and ceremonial. Here the Khedive spends the day transacting various business, seeing ministers, reading letters and telegrams, and talking with his courtiers. At five o'clock in the evening he drives out again accompanied by his guards, and dines about sunset at Ismailia.

I well remember my first dinner with the Khedive. One enters the palace by a lofty arched gateway between high walls, which inclose a beautiful garden. On either side of the gateway is a sort of colonnade and verandah, with rooms opening upon it: it is in these rooms that the Court officials reside on the rare occasions when the Khedive stays at home for the day. In the garden are palms and bananas, bourgainvillia, poinsettia, hibiscus, and many other shrubs and flowers of great brilliance. A double flight of white marble steps leads up from the garden to the central hall of the palace. Around this hall are saloons furnished in European fashion. We dined at an oval table. The Khedive always sits in the centre of one of the longer sides, with a vacant space right and left: the places nearest him were occupied by two of the chief pashas, such as the Keeper of the Seals and the Grand Master of the Ceremonies; then came the rest of the company in order of dignity. On this occasion there were seven pashas present, besides Turâbi Bey and Tonino Bey. The Khedive spoke chiefly in French, which no one present understood except Tonino and myself, and described with great animation his reception of the sacred camel, which had returned with the pilgrims from Mecca that morning. "That," he said, "is a ceremony of great importance in our religion, and I encourage it; it is harmless and involves no sort of practice that is barbarous or revolting. But in a few days you will see another ceremony about which I have a different opinion, the Dôsah, or Trampling of the Dervishes; it is an inhuman rite, but it does not seem possible to stop it."

When dinner is over the Khedive leads the way

across the hall to another saloon. "Neshûfkom" (we will see you) is the usual invitation to the company to follow. The guests sit on a row of stiff-backed chairs across the middle of the room, facing the Khedive; His Highness reclines in a low easy seat and leads the conversation. Whenever I was present, English or French was spoken nearly the whole evening, and the pashas had a dull time. Coffee and cigarettes were always brought by black servants; on receiving either it is customary to salute one's host, though not in any ostentatious manner. When our cigarettes were finished, we all retired, passed across the garden to the anterooms, and there waited; then, if there was no pressing business to engage the Khedive, he sent an orderly to summon any one with whom he wished to have private conversation. I shall have some of these private interviews to record hereafter.

The Dôsah, of which mention has been made, was part of the celebration of the Mûlid-en-Nebi, or Prophet's Birthday. The festival occupies several days, and was usually held on a great open space near the English church. Tents are arranged upon it in the form of a large square, each tent belonging to some great sheikh and his following of dervishes;

there is also a splendid tent belonging to the Khedive, and another set apart for the Court.

Every night for a week great rejoicings are held; Muslims come from all parts to see their friends and to be present at the solemn "zikrs," or services of prayer, at which the devotees are wrought up to a strange pitch of religious excitement; moreover, fireworks and other amusements are furnished. The Dôsah came on the last day—this year a Sunday. Though the ceremony was thus the most striking feature of the greatest religious festival of Egypt, it did not date back further than two centuries. The theory of it was that no good and true dervish could suffer hurt or pain under any torture of the body enjoined by his religion.

I went down to the encampment about eleven o'clock that morning, and sat in the Court tent talking with my companions. We were on the western side of the square down which the great procession was to pass. Opposite our line of tents, and divided by a clear course forty feet in width, was a dense throng of carriages and people. The course was kept by soldiers; it reached from the entrance of the grounds to the tent of the chief dervish, a distance of three hundred yards; and a piece of matting ten feet wide was spread the whole way. On this matting the devotees were to lie prostrate while the sheikh on horseback rode over them.

About noon the Khedive arrived, and alighted at his tent. Soon afterwards a confused murmur arose, announcing that the procession of dervishes was coming. A few moments more and one saw in the distance a line of banners moving forwards, their red and green pennons embroidered with texts from the Korân. Most of the dervishes were turbaned and robed in the usual Arab fashion, while others wore strange dresses distinctive of special tribes. Some had shaven heads, with a tuft of long hair on the crown; others had masses of mane tossing about their shoulders. Some few wore mail-armour; some were naked down to the waist. As they entered the course the foremost broke into a run, or rather staggered and plunged along, their bodies swaying, their eyes rolling, and mouths foaming like madmen. Many could not stand without help: others, with frantic violence, were crushing live serpents in their hands or tearing them to pieces with their teeth and devouring them ravenously: some were eating glass and fire: some were thrusting spikes of steel clean through their cheeks and arms: some were wildly beating tom-toms or shaking rattles: some were gashing their faces and breasts with knives and scimetars, while others merely carried a sword with the edge laid against the throat, in calmer symbolism of self-sacrifice. All, however, seemed wrought up to a mad frenzy of religious excitement, aided by a powerful drug called hashish; all were literally raving, roaring, and gnashing their teeth. It was a dreadful and revolting spectacle, but worse was to follow.

As each set reached its place, a signal was given, and they fell violently down on their faces upon the matting. Now came their officers and packed them all close together, side by side, as they lay at full length, so as to leave no space between the bodies. The poor wretches were quivering, foaming, and muttering "Allah! Allah!" between clenched teeth. The attendants took off every man's slippers and placed them under his face; they also dressed the line of prostrate figures, seizing here and there a man by the heels and pulling him a little, so that the trunks of the bodies should lie quite even and make a broad pavement for the horse, which was to be kept off the neck and legs. This done, the dervishes became somewhat more quiet; their heads moved less, and rested on the crossed arms, face downwards; but the hideous moans continued. When the line had thus been finally arranged, the horse carrying the sheikh of all the dervishes started. The sheikh wore an enormous green turban, a snuff-coloured robe, and variegated girdle. A man at each side walked leading the horse by the bridle; two others walked beside the sheikh to hold him on; for his eyes were closed, and he reeled in the saddle, overcome with excitement. Just in front of the horse a man ran over the bodies, and two others some way ahead moved shouting a warning to the prostrate forms to be ready, for the sheikh was coming. He was a big man, and the horse was a stout cob—altogether a terrible weight to ride over a road of human flesh.

As I stood actually in front of the Khedive's tent upon the matting, my feet touching the line of heads, I could see with horrible clearness all that happened. Many of the poor wretches had friends squatting before them and fanning their sunken faces; but no voice or sound was uttered among them. I saw the dreaded horse approaching, and a crowd following at the side, raising a strange excited clamour. As the horse neared me, a frightened dervish sprang up and ran away, but another was promptly seized from the crowd and flung down in his place. Now I watched every footfall of the horse; for I was determined to know the truth, and to report it. Many of the natives had told me that the horse did not tread on the bodies, but merely stepped across them, planting his feet between. This I soon saw was false; the bodies were packed so close that the horse *must* trample upon them.

On he came. I saw the dreadful yielding of the bodies, as thigh or ribs, spine or shoulder, felt the crushing weight of the hoofs, and I saw the writhing of the poor tortured forms. Just opposite me the horse planted his foot on the side of a poor wretch and let it slip down between two men; the result was that he stumbled, plunged heavily forward, recovered with difficulty, and came with dreadful force on one or two bodies before my very eyes. I set my teeth, furious with indignation, and vowed that this should never happen again; while in a carriage opposite a party of Europeans were laughing loud, as if the thing were a joke. I am glad that they were not English.

So the horse moved on, mangling the bodies beneath his feet. For a moment after he passed the dervishes lay still; all bore the first shock in silence, for this is the proof of their faith. But after an instant's pause all rose or tried to rise. Some were unhurt and jumped up pell-mell; others, as they tried to move, shrieked, and yelled, and fell back fainting. It was an awful sight; forms half-lifeless, with fixed eyes, dropped jaw, protruding tongue; others writhing and plunging in pain. The physical torture one witnessed, the dark faces whitened with anguish, made one sick with horror and pity. But friends and comrades crowded round and hurried the victims off the scene. The wounded are sent away from Cairo, and the dead are buried secretly, and no one ever knows the number of either, lest it should be said that the Prophet's miracle was not accomplished. Accordingly the natives believe that no one ever is hurt.*

But when the sheikh had ridden over the line, he returned another way to the Khedive's tent, where he was pulled off his horse and mumbled a prayer; but he met with a cold reception. As he retired again, a crowd thronged round him, eager to touch

* I may quote a curiously exact parallel from Herodotus. Speaking of the religious procession and fight at Papremis, he says—καὶ, ὡς ἐγὼ δοκέω, πολλοὶ καὶ ἀποθνήσκουσι ἐκ τῶν τρωμάτων· οὐ μέντοι οἵ γε Αἰγύπτιοι ἔφασαν ἀποθνήσκειν οὐδένα. (Book ii. chapter 63.)

the holy man, and kissing the hand of any one who touched him. Such is the indifference to brutality produced by fanaticism.

I should mention that, while the sheikh was in the Khedive's tent, I went to have a close look at the horse. It was not a large one, judging by English standards; but a good size for an Arab, and shod in the manner of the country, *i.e.*, with a disc of iron covering the whole under-surface of the hoof. Natives had assured me that the horse was not shod at all: but again their information was wrong. During the ceremony the Khedive remained in his tent, preferring to see little or nothing of the barbarities enacted. But I left the scene resolving that he should at least know the whole truth about the Dôsah, resolving also that I would never rest until the Dôsah was abolished.

Directly after this tragic scene, I was glad to get a day away from Cairo, and resolved to go with my Oxford friend A—— up country to visit the curious pyramid of Maidûm. We were to start from the hotel with daylight, and had ordered two days' provisions: but when the hour came not a single thing was ready: the porter had clean forgotten the order. With great exertions we got some cold meats, bread, wine, coffee, and oranges tumbled into a hamper, and, driving fast through the white morning mists, just caught the train at Bulâk ed Dakrûr. Reaching Wasta, we could get nothing better to mount us and our servant than three miserable donkeys, unadorned even with a halter for bridle, or a mat for saddle. But we paid for them as if they were pashas' pet asses, some of which are splendid animals, and fetch 120*l*. a piece ; for a pasha, especially if stout and comfortable, prefers the peaceable even gait of a donkey to the spirited paces of a charger.

Besides the donkeys we had also to hire four men as guards: one carried an ancient musket, the rest sticks, and the only danger they could possibly deliver us from was a superfluity of provisions. We laid our ulsters across the donkeys for saddles ; and I carried my gun across my saddle-bows, when I was not using it to guide my beast. Our path lay over a great plain of tillage covered with the richest verdure. We lunched in some standing corn, and paid the owner a franc for the damage ; then on again past the picturesque village of Maidûm to the pyramid, which lies some way beyond on the margin of the desert.

There too our guide-book had spoken of "a street of empty tombs," in one of which we meant to camp for the night, having brought no tents. But the description was drawn from imagination, and we could find no shelter but a sort of open doorway or portico eight feet high, ten feet long, and five broad. This proved to be the entrance to the closed tomb of Nefermat, a building older than the great pyramid of Gizah, perhaps the earliest monument in Egypt with name and date at all assignable. It was from a tomb near this that the pair of statues representing Rahotep and his wife were taken—the oldest stone statues in the world, perhaps the most wonderful objects amid the wonders of the Bulâk museum. We spread a carpet in the portico and lay down, while 'Ali made coffee: then we walked to the pyramid, which differs from other pyramids in rising by terraces and in being unfinished. Moreover it has never been opened: the secret of its five thousand years remains inviolate. But the bees had frayed the surface of the huge fabric with their tiny cells, and chameleons darted about the crevices of the stones.

The pyramid, as I have mentioned, and the tomb, stood at the edge of the desert, on an elevated plateau overlooking eastward the green plains watered by the Nile: while westward stretched the untravelled sands of the Sahara. At the foot of this

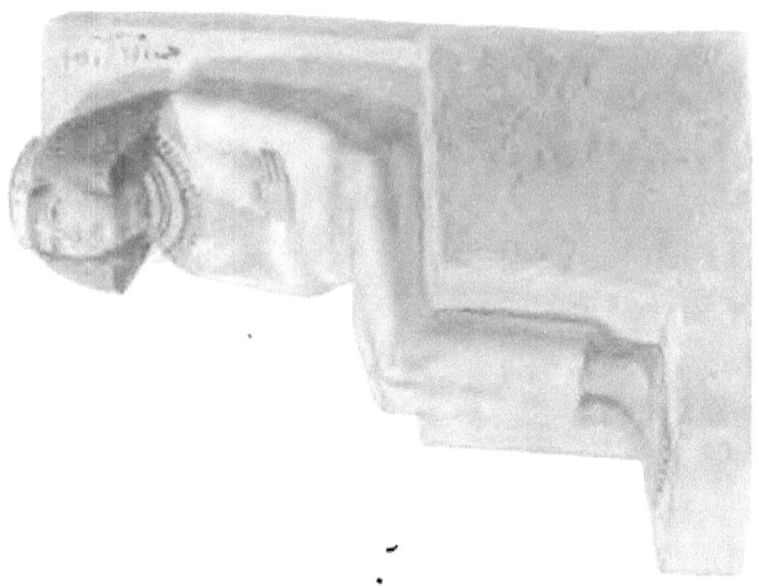

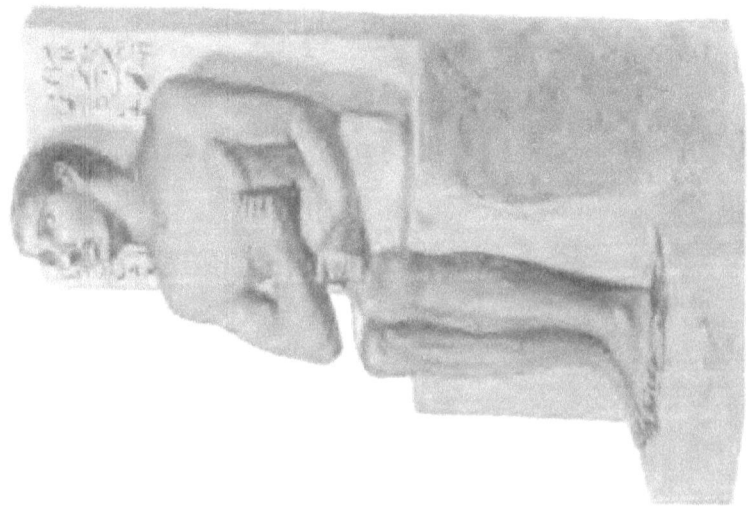

plateau was a dyke or canal, for ages out of use, but still half filled with water. Wild fowl abounded, and towards sunset when they were on the wing I sallied out, hoping to get a duck for our dinner. But there was not an atom of covert, and no chance of getting a shot from ambush, while the ducks were much too wary to come within range. But we fared well enough, and after dinner sat in our tomb smoking and talking, moralising on the historic site we were profaning, and rekindling classic memories of philosophers and poets.

But I had not done with the ducks. So at ten o'clock, under a glorious full moon, I took my gun and revolver; for 'Ali was strangely depressed, and seemed to have a fixed idea that we should be attacked. For two full hours I wandered along the canal, crouching whenever I heard a noise of beating wings, and trying to stalk any birds I saw on the water. Once, in the distance, I spied a huge flock of wild geese, their white plumage gleaming in the still moonlight. With beating heart I crawled slowly and stealthily on all fours, falling flat at the least alarm. My hopes were rising; I neglected an easy shot at a stray duck, and was now within a hundred and fifty yards of the geese, when with a furious clangour of wings and cackle they rose and swept far away out of sight.

Before I could recover the shock of chagrin, there leapt out of the darkness a tall white-robed Beduin, who stood at a little distance gesticulating savagely, shouting, and aiming a long gun at me point-blank. Not knowing in the least what he was so angry about, I merely glanced at my hammers and stood waiting. We now saw that there were three or four Beduins, all rather wild about something or other. My companion and I both carried revolvers, but neither felt very comfortable. Fortunately at the critical moment one of our guard, who had been following unknown to us at a distance, came running up, and after some vigorous language on both sides succeeded in calming the Beduins. It seemed that they had a sheepfold beside the water, though it was hidden from our view by a ridge of sand; and that, seeing me crawling along the bank with a gun and approaching them with the utmost stealth and precaution, they had concluded that our purpose was to surprise them and lift their cattle. I thought it just as well that the geese had risen when they did, relieving me of the need of concealment. Had I gone much further in the same manner, no doubt a bullet or two without warning would have whistled about my ears, and the result would have been a painful, though possibly brief, astonishment.

It was now late and time to return. On the way back I got but one shot, and dropped a duck in the water. In point of sport the midnight expedition was a failure. When we got home to our tomb, we lay down well wrapped in rugs and ulsters, while our guards sat crouching and chattering incessantly at the entrance. What with the cold and the noise sound sleep was impossible; one fell into a kind of dozing state, wherein a murmur of voices was always present. In this condition of lowered consciousness a strange thing happened; for I clearly remember overhearing our Arab guards holding long conversations and speaking apparently in good English, though they knew not a word of that language. At the time I was too dreamy even to feel surprised; but in the morning I mentioned the fact to my companion, and found that he had had the same curious experience. As the number of sounds in any language is limited, it may be that the half-awakened brain selected enough familiar sounds for the imagination to weave together: but of this I am certain, that it was not a mere dream and illusion of slumber.

Just before sunrise I tried the duck again, but vainly; then we walked to the pyramid, where the hum of myriad bees awakening from their cells upon the fretted surface of the stone resounded like a morning hymn—a hymn sung in greeting of the sun, then just mounting over the eastern hills. When the bright globe had fully risen, the music ceased and the bees dispersed over the clover plains. Is it possible, I wondered, in like manner to explain by the humming of bees the legendary music of Memnon?

Charmed with the sound and scene we wandered back to breakfast and found 'Ali in a good humour again, as the night was passed in safety. Then, turning westward, we went for a long stroll in the desert. The surface here was hard and dark, covered with small pebbles of various colours; but when we had traversed some distance there flashed into view a most beautiful mirage. Not half a mile in front of us we saw pools and lakes of clear blue glistening water, varied with capes and bays and set with lovely islands. Already the sun was exceedingly hot, and the vision made one long to drink. Finding that the scene shifted as one approached, I resolved to fix my eyes on a single point and walk deliberately up to it. As I drew near, the panorama gradually lessened, while lakes, islands, palms, and promontories slowly passed from view, till there remained only a single sheet of water with an ever-narrowing margin. Still the borders closed in, till, at a few paces distant, nothing was left but a tiny pool; and as I advanced, this too vanished away, leaving nothing but sand to mark its place. Then I lifted up my eyes and saw on the horizon the deceitful vision, fair as ever. Whatever may be the right explanation of the mirage, this, I think, was not the reflection of any scene in Egypt.

On our return we saw some peasants carting hewn stones from the base of the pyramid—a process which seemed to have been going on for some time. Towards afternoon we mounted our beasts and made for the Nile, where we enjoyed a bathe, though the current is too swift for any lengthened stay in the water. We reached Cairo without incident. Two days later I reported to the Khedive the destruction going on at the Maidûm pyramid; he was pleased at being told, and promised to send strict orders to the mudir to stop the practice.

Early in March the Khedive gave a State ball at the palace of 'Abdin. Of course this sort of ceremony is too public for native ladies; but all the chief resident Europeans are invited, and the Khedive, with all his Court, pashas, officers, and ministers, is present. The splendid saloons of the palace are thrown open. Though the furniture is all French, some idea of its magnificence may be formed from the fact that even in the anterooms each pair of curtains cost about 60*l*. It goes without saying, that this extravagance lies at Ismail's door: the present Khedive would not and could not spend money in so reckless a fashion.

But the sumptuousness of the palace furniture was almost equalled by that of the ladies' dresses: silks of the most gorgeous hue and most costly fabric, priceless laces, jewels of oriental size and brilliance. Many of the ladies were young and very beautiful, especially the Italians and Syrians: but nearly all were married. Dancing took place in one saloon only. Round the walls stood a ring of beys and pashas three deep, mostly Turkish, Arab, and Circassian officers, who watched the scene with the air of men looking at performing monkeys, and made rude but deserved remarks on the extraordinary lowness of the ladies' dresses. One good Turk, married to a very stout lady who happened to be present, took me by the arm and whispered, "Mr. Butler, I want you to dance with my wife. She is here, but I don't allow her to dance with these fellows. I trust you; she shall dance with no one else but you. Come and be introduced; she loves dancing." I was caught, and escape was impossible. Her forehead, for all I know, may have been like a glorious planet, her eyebrows like the new moon of Ramadhan, her mouth like Solomon's seal, and her teeth a mockery to the reason of poet and prose-writer; but her form was *not* like the letter Alif, nor her figure like a sprig of oriental willow.* Indeed the good lady was terribly heavy, and had no idea of moving *proprio motu:* it was like dancing with a huge pillar of granite, and the heat of the room was unbearable. After the second dance with her I retired, aching in every bone, to the supper-room, where the Khedive himself was dispensing hospitality. For the rest of the evening I took care to be two rooms off both my Turkish friend and his spouse. Besides talking to the Khedive a good deal, I here met his brother, Mahmûd Bey, for the first time.

Mahmûd has few of the Khedive's good qualities,

---

* Common expressions with the Arabs denoting grace and beauty.

neither his strength of good purpose, nor his cleverness, nor his charming gift of manner. He would talk by the hour about military engineering and the like, but with little intelligence, and little coherence. His marriage, owing to peculiar reasons, had turned out a very unsuccessful affair. But that story is a ἱερὸς λόγος, and, like Herodotus, I may say that I know it well, but forget it on purpose; yet it is very curious and quite as remarkable as anything in the Arabian Nights; moreover it has been confirmed to me by all the authorities. Mahmûd Bey talked English very fairly; he had been Turâbi's pupil, and had proved rather a handful.

The weather now turned cold and cloudy, and was as unpleasant as it was unusual. It culminated on March 15th in a hailstorm, which greatly puzzled the Arabs. I overheard a discussion in which one man said the hailstones were pebbles. "Wallâhi," said another, "these are no stones; they are grains of salt." "Son of a donkey," said a third, "taste it; it is sweet. By the head of my father, this is rice." And the matter was settled by "Mâ sh' allah! it is rice, mâ sh' allah! Verily this is an event to be recorded in books!"

But the sun returned, and the days rolled on. All

this time I heard nothing of my rooms or my pupils. But there was plenty of amusement at the Court and in the bazaars. One day I was sitting watching a silversmith at work, and expressed interest in a curious silver wand which he was making. On the top of it were two doves facing each other, and it was hung with little bells. A pretty Arab girl was bargaining for it, and in reply to my questions she told me that it was for driving away the devil. Can this be a tradition from the sistrum? Many curious relics of ancient Egyptian custom may undoubtedly be found among the Copts and Arabs. Thus they think it very unlucky to hurt or kill an ibis; and Herodotus relates that the punishment for killing an ibis by design or accident was death. The killing of an ox before the Khedive's carriage seems a similar reminiscence; similar also is the custom for women at a funeral to smear mud upon their heads and bosoms.*

Besides the new things that one saw, there were many strange stories to hear, and men more or less famous to meet. About this time I met Captain Burton, whose marvellous knowledge of eastern life and languages must alone make him a unique figure,

---

* See Herodotus, book ii. chapter 85.

even were he not a brilliant talker and the hero of the daring pilgrimage to Mecca. I met him dining at Turâbi's house, and Turâbi afterwards told me that he was on board the same ship with Captain Burton bound for Alexandria, when the latter was about starting on his great journey. Turâbi was struck with the regularity and earnestness with which a certain poorly-dressed Arab performed his devotions, and watching him rather narrowly suddenly recognised his friend Captain Burton. A burst of laughter followed; but Burton, seeing his disguise penetrated, merely made a quick sign of silence, and went on with his prayers. Turâbi took the hint, but subsequently they had many a chat in private, and the good little Turk was of service to the Englishman in his initiation as Musulman.

Many of the stories which I heard about the Court related to a certain person called Naib es Sultânah. One in particular made a great impression on me, and, though at the time I could scarcely believe it, I give it for what it is worth. Naib es Sultânah's greatest friend and most trusted agent was a man named Ismail Pasha Sâdik, who held the position of Mufettish, or Finance Minister. The Mufettish kept a full chest, always knew where money was, and how to raise it. Naib would send a message: "I want so much," and the Mufettish ordered the Mudirs to bring in the amount. Of course the Mudirs profited by the process, while by thumbscrew and kûrbash the uttermost farthing was wrung from the miserable fellahin. If a fellah spent a little money, the Mudir pounced upon him, and, charging him with the crime of wealth, imprisoned and flogged him till he confessed and surrendered his hoard. Many pots full of gold undoubtedly lie under the soil, where the owners buried them and died with their secret untold and undiscovered. Well, when a Frankish gentleman came out to Egypt as Finance Commissioner, Naib took alarm, knowing that his books were not kept in a way to invite inspection. So he first of all drained the Treasury by distributing no less a sum than 1,000,000*l.* sterling amongst the harims. The ready money thus secured, his next move was to destroy the records of his extortion and extravagance. His quick mind saw that this meant, in fact, the destruction of the Mufettish, who was certain to be cross-examined, and whose evidence would be most damning. It was his nature to decide resolutely and to act swiftly. Still some caution was necessary. The Mufettish lived in state and splendour scarcely inferior to that of his sovereign; it would not do to clap him in prison. So Naib drove in his carriage to the Ministry of Finance, and, sending for the Mufettish, said, "My dear friend, I want to have a good talk with you; step into my carriage and we will go together to call on Amîr at Gezirah." My informant beheld the two men chatting as the carriage swept past his windows, but the Mufettish was never seen again.

This is what happened. When they reached Gezirah, they alighted together and walked into the palace. Naib preceded his friend by a few paces, and as soon as he had passed out of the hall, a guard sprang forward and seized the pasha. "What is this?" he exclaimed in astonishment, "what are you doing?" For reply he received a blow in the face. Amîr, who was privy to the plot, ordered him to be thrown into a dungeon. Thence he was taken at night, placed on a steamer, strangled, and sunk in the Nile.

The steamer, however, with a guard on board went on its way southwards, for Naib gave out next day that the Mufettish had been banished to the White Nile, and the steamer was sent to give colour to the rumour. No boat was allowed to come near the steamer, even with fresh provisions, under pain of being fired upon. Nevertheless the Mufettish was not on board: his lifeless body was lying at the bottom of the river. When the steamer arrived at Wadi Halfa, it is certain that no Mufettish landed, and there was no Mufettish in the caravan that crossed the desert from Korosko to Abu Hamed. What is more, not a single soldier of the guard has ever returned to Cairo or been heard of since. Dead men tell no tales.

Yet the story of the banishment was circulated and ostentatiously inserted even in Turkish papers. Soon the same journals began to inform the public that the poor Mufettish had taken to drinking in his exile, and within a few months they recorded his death from drunkenness. No one in Egypt however was deceived by this elaborate fiction. There the truth was known and had a standing witness in Is'hâk Bey's mutilated hand. For Is'hâk Bey was the chief agent in the actual murder, and the old Mufettish, when he saw that his hour was come, did not die without a struggle. He fought for his life as best he could, and in course of the scuffle bit off one of Is'hâk Bey's fingers. No ignominy attached to Is'hâk, who was retained in the service of Prince Mahmûd till just before my visit to Egypt; it was said that he had merely obeyed orders under compulsion. But when the present Khedive came to the throne, he thought it discreditable that a man with the stain of blood upon him should have a post of honour about the Prince his brother; so Is'hâk was dismissed. But he was still to be seen about Cairo in my time, and his maimed hand was conspicuous.

Such is the history of that most foul and treacherous murder, a history to which I shall have to recur again hereafter. Now let me tell some tales of a less tragic kind about the same person. From Naib's accounts, which fell ultimately into the hands of the Controllers, it appears that in one year he laid hands on and squandered 3,500,000*l.*, all state money belonging to the Treasury. His form of draft was, "Pay bearer 100,000*l.* : by order." The draft was presented at the Treasury and paid forthwith. In bribery of various kinds he spent no less than 40,000,000*l.*; of this 12,000,000*l.* went to the Sultan and 6,000,000*l.* among a great number of European journals, including some English newspapers. Moreover, while professing devotion to the Sultan, Naib really intrigued for his overthrow, and, amongst his other projects, he secretly aided the insurrection in

CALIFORNIA

MUSHRABIAH WINDOW IN CAIRO

Crete, to which he gave altogether 3,000,000*l*. These figures seem incredible, but I believe them to be correct. The Opera House in Cairo cost him the modest sum of 60,000*l*. to build, but in one season of five months' duration he spent 120,000*l*. upon the company. One actress alone got 1200*l*. a month; all had money and jewels showered on them at leaving. The scenery, costumes, and *mise-en-scène* generally were of an unheard-of magnificence.

The site for the Opera House and the adjoining Esbekiah gardens was obtained in a very characteristic manner. It was occupied by old Arab houses, closely packed in the fashion of the native quarter. Compensation was offered for surrender, and those of the freeholders or leaseholders who accepted it cleared out, and the abandoned buildings were pulled down. Many tenants however rejected the offer, which was by no means liberal. Thereupon Naib ordered their houses to be secretly set on fire: and, when they were burnt down, he sent to condole with the tenants on their misfortune, and generously renewed his offer of compensation, which was accepted. This is a type of Naib's dealing—very clever, but utterly unscrupulous.

At the beginning of April there came a sudden

order for me to move into my rooms at 'Abdin palace. I found a spacious suite of rooms at my disposal, on the whole well furnished: but there were some very startling exceptions. Divans, carpets, curtains, mirrors, &c. were all very fine: but the dust and dirt of the place were unspeakable. Nearly three months were supposed to have been spent in "getting the rooms ready": it was quite clear they had been opened that morning and not so much as dusted. The bed consisted of one blanket and one sheet: the mosquito-curtains were in rags. Towards evening my request for towels was answered: *one* was produced, very dirty, and with a hole two feet long down the middle. The Khedive, as Turâbi told me, had given orders for everything to be done for my comfort; dinner would be served at seven o'clock. I sat reading and waiting till long after eight, and then was told "There is no dinner to-night, but it will be all right to-morrow." I went out and dined at the hotel.

The next two days I lived mostly at the hotel, while my rooms were really being made ready for my reception. When the Khedive heard how his instructions had been carried out, he was very angry and gave instant orders that whatever I required I written demand was to be furnished new forthwith. This was done. I heard, however, that the Marshal of the Palace, Yûsif Pasha, on reading the modest demand for a dozen towels, had remarked, "God is great, and what God pleases happens: but what in God's name can he do with twelve towels?" Yûsif, from his slavish origin, had very native ideas. But at last I was established in comfort, though the rooms had a south and west aspect, and my friends cheerfully remarked, "You will be grilled in the summer." As for meals, coffee was served in the morning early, lunch at noon, and dinner at sunset: the latter hours were marked every day by the boom of a gun from the citadel.

I spoke just now of living in comfort; but the term is relative. To the last I could never abide the native cookery. My lunch and dinner were brought in a circular wooden tray, which a tall white-robed Arab carried on his head; the tray was covered with a great straw dome, beneath which rested five or six small round dishes, while over it was spread an embroidered covering. Sometimes it would happen that the dishes contained edible food, and on bright particular occasions even a pleasant repast; but far more often, as dish after dish was set before me, I dismissed it with a wave of the hand and a "shil"* to my servant. Then if I had time, or if it were not too insufferably hot, I would go to the hotel; but many and many a time my dinner consisted of six "shils" followed by some dry biscuits. The wine, however, was excellent. Most of the officials of the palace messed together except the few who always sat down with the Khedive. But as the mess was very promiscuous, and included some with whom I did not care to associate as equals, I refused to join it. The Khedive's orders were that my table should be the same as his own; of course they were not carried out. But it was wiser not to complain in such a matter.

* *i. e.* Take it away.

CHAPTER III.

Journey in Lower Egypt—Sulimân—Dinner with 'Abdu 'l 'Al— Ruins at Thmuis—Damietta—Zagazig—Miseries of Tantah— The sirocco—Encounter with a lunatic—Rosetta—Smelling the zephyr.

As the Khedive's progress in Upper Egypt had been judged a great success, he determined to follow it up forthwith by a similar journey through Lower Egypt or the Delta. To me the news was very welcome; obviously it was great fortune to get such a chance of seeing almost the whole of Egypt within four months of my arrival in the country. Just before we started, the Court was surprised by the sudden dismissal of the Austrian aide-de-camp. I called on him to offer my condolences, being extremely sorry to lose so pleasant and gentlemanly a companion in our travels. At his rooms I met a compatriot of his, Count ———, who was very indignant, and exclaimed,

F

"When the English flag is hoisted in Egypt, I shall be the first to salute it." It is a curious question whether that salute has ever been given.

Our expedition left Kasr-en-nil by steamer on April 10th, and reached Benha that evening. There all the notables of the province had assembled and pitched their tents, which were illuminated with lanterns. We went about at night from tent to tent drinking ceremonial coffee and smoking peaceable pipes. But Benha had no great attractions. It is remarkable, however, for its pigeons; for the natives build whole villages of pigeon-towers, each tower being a lofty cone about fifty feet high and ten feet in diameter at the base. Scores of these, all clustered together, are haunted by thousands of pigeons.

The next day brought a furious sirocco, and at noon, while we were at luncheon with the Khedive, we were beset by a plague of hornets; but, unless provoked, these beasts are more alarming than harmful. The thermometer was at 105° in the shade, a degree of heat which on board ship is terrible, especially in a cabin which faces the afternoon sun. A swim in the river gives little or no relief. After two days more of this weather, when we had reached Samanûd, the sirocco ceased and the north wind blew cool again.

Samanûd, the old Sebennytus, was the birthplace of Manetho, and once a town of some note, now a collection of hovels. There being nothing else to do, I went out shooting on an island in the river with Goudard Bey. For the quail were passing northward at this time, and with them the beautiful bee-eaters, which the Italians call "king of the quail," the French, "syrens." I was anxious to obtain some specimens, and in less than an hour shot seven. They are rather shy birds, but by good luck I made a right and left at such a range that the Frenchman refused to shoot any longer or do anything but follow me about with exclamations of amazement. My servant Sulimân undertook to skin the birds with his usual dexterity, but alas! before we reached Cairo again, the rats had eaten up the skins.

Sulimân has had a very adventurous life, and though still young is now quite a historical character. He is a Sudanese by parentage, but lived as a boy in Alexandria, where he very early ran away from his father, and commenced to earn his own living by his wits. He even contrived to educate himself, so that, beside his native language, he learned to read and write good Arabic, an accomplishment not possessed by one servant in five hundred. He entered Sir Samuel Baker's service and accompanied his exploring expedition up the Nile. His name is mentioned in "Ismailia," * and Sulimân takes pride in pointing out the passages: for among his many accomplishments he talks English and even reads a little. It will be seen presently that I had to part with Sulimân ere many months were over, but I did so with regret. Just before I quitted Egypt I was pleased to have the chance of recommending him as chief servant to Mr. James, who was about starting for his Sudân expedition. He proved an invaluable servant, and is spoken of in the highest terms in Mr. James's well-known account of his travels.† Early in 1884, when I was again in Cairo, I was one day greeted with beaming smiles and salâms by a richly-clad figure, which started up from a gateway which I happened to be passing. It was Sulimân, who had at once recognised me, and who was then in the distinguished service of General Stephenson, Commander of the British Army of Occupation. Sulimân looked supremely happy; he told me that he had enjoyed his Sudân travels very much indeed, and had subse-

* "Ismailia," vol. i. p. 209, &c. (1874).
† "Wild Tribes of the Soudan," by F. L. James, pp. 262-3 (1883).

quently been taken to England by Mr. James; the English climate, however, did not agree with him and he was glad to get back to Cairo. The splendour of his attire bespoke a comfortable position, which doubtless he still adorns.

But to return from this digression. An amusing incident happened at Samanûd. We had on board our steamer a certain Mustapha Pasha, an extremely pious Musulman, who, unlike many of his brethren, never forgot his prayers. At sunset on the evening of our arrival his servant brought his prayer-carpet up to spread upon the deck; but just as the pasha was making ready for his first posture, it occurred to him that his servant had not got the right orientation for the carpet. The river here winds somewhat, so that it really was difficult to find the true east. Poor Mustapha was turning about in helpless bewilderment, fixing the direction every minute only to alter it. I saw his perplexity, and, happening to have a small compass, went up to him and gave him his bearings, for which he was grateful; and I left him bowing his devotions in peace.

Our evening meal here gave me my first experience of a native dinner. We were guests of a certain 'Abdu 'l 'Al Bey, who became afterwards one of the three ringleaders in 'Arâbi's rebellion. We sat at a round table, with no plates, knives, or forks. Dish after dish was placed in the centre, and all dived into it with their fingers. The Homeric line

$$οἱ δ' ἐπ' ὀνείαθ' ἑτοῖμα προχείμενα χεῖρας ἴαλλον$$

was henceforth clothed with a vivid and indelible meaning.

Mansûra, our next station, is a town of some pretension. It has a mosque associated with the captivity of St. Louis in the year 1250; but as a rule these Delta towns, and their buildings, are rather uninteresting. The whole bank of the river opposite our steamer was set with a continuous arcading of painted woodwork, hung with flags and lanterns innumerable. We had endless native music by day, and fireworks by night; but the whole affair was rather tedious. Accordingly, as we had a clear day to spend here, I set off with Sulimân the morning after our arrival, intending to reach the little-known ruins of Mendes.

From the outset I suspected that our direction was wrong; but Sulimân had made all possible inquiries, and was sure the Arabs knew of no ruins in the neighbourhood except those to which we were going. It was a very long but pleasant ride. I lunched about midday, Sulimân holding an umbrella over me, —the only kind of shadow obtainable in the dead level of the treeless plain. At 2·30 we reached vast mounds of rubbish which proved to be the remains of the ancient Thmuis. There was a little village by them, and the villagers had some antiques; but unfortunately my khedivial uniform frightened them into an obstinate refusal even to show their treasures. After wandering over the rubbish mounds and finding some beautiful fragments of ancient glass and pottery, I made for a ruin distant about a mile and bearing the name of Kasr el Far'aun, *i. e.* Pharaoh's Castle or Palace. The ruin is curious, and does not appear to be noticed in the guide-books. All that now remains is a gigantic shrine of red syenite; it stands on a broad pedestal formed by six courses of stone, each course no less than three feet in thickness, and towers in solitary grandeur above the plain. The sub-structure is in a broken and imperfect condition; and the drifted sand and soil about the base help further to conceal the purpose of this strange monument. It is unlike anything else which I have seen in Egypt, and deserves exploration. No other relics were visible except a number of enormous granite vessels, like baths or troughs, each hewn out of a solid block. These lie about at random, and are as puzzling as the architectural remains.

A ride through the Delta, away from the beaten tracks, is quite worth making. There, far more even than in the towns along the Nile-banks, one finds the true fellah—the veritable Egyptian of ancient times — with customs and manners little changed from those of four or five thousand years ago. On my way back I saw women working in the fields, and men spinning, just as Herodotus notices.*

I was much struck too by the walk and carriage of the peasants, more especially of the women; it is magnificent. A woman seldom walks arm in arm with a man, but rests her hand on his shoulder,— a much more graceful attitude. It was long after sunset when I reached our steamer again. I was taken to task for having travelled such a distance across country without my revolver; but in those days Egypt was as safe for travel as England. Now, thanks to three years of British rule, based on the principle of doing no good and suffering all evil,

* Herodotus, book ii. chapter 35.

that once peaceable country is as dangerous as the wilds of Turkestan.*

From Mansûra we continued down the river amid improving scenery. The country is as flat as Port Meadow, but the villages are very pretty, and mostly adorned with mosques and minarets. Damietta was reached ere noon—a town beautifully situated at a bend of the river, which here opens out to a great breadth. The houses are mostly on the eastern bank, and follow the sweeping curve of the water. Few of the buildings are modern or European: most are extremely picturesque examples of old "Arab," or rather Coptic, architecture. The minarets are specially fine: the designs of the carved stonework on these and on the great doorways being remarkable for grace and delicacy. Gardens of palm stand round the ancient city in refreshing contrast to the time-worn piles of building.

In the afternoon I walked down to the shores of Lake Menzâleh with my gun, on the chance of a shot at wild fowl, with which the lake abounds. But I saw no birds along the shore, and the only boats obtainable were the giant barges that ply under sail

---

* It is only fair to state that, since the above words were written, brigands have been repressed, and travel made comparatively safe.

across the water. Most of these too were lying deep embedded in the mud, like rotting hulks of some abandoned harbour. The dazzling silver surface of the lake gleamed unruffled by a breath of wind, unbroken by any stir of life: the very reeds seemed asleep: and the place might have been an enchanted mere in a fairy land but for the abominable odour which arose from the shore, and soon sent one flying helter-skelter away. Towards evening the Khedive and Court called upon a rich merchant named Hajji Said el Luzi, who has a large house in the town. The courtyard was illuminated with fifteen hundred lamps; carpets were spread for the Khedive to walk on, and rose-leaves were scattered before his feet; while bands of native music charmed the oriental ear.

Damietta, once a thriving seaport with a vast trade, is now some leagues distant from the sea, and inaccessible to ships of large burden. This change is owing of course to the action of the Nile, which forms a vast deposit at its mouth.

The day after our arrival we went down in our steamers to the sea and landed on the western promontory. It was curious to see the big pashas, with their trailing swords, trotting and rushing about like

EGYPTIAN SALUTE.

children, digging the sand and picking up pebbles and shells. After an hour's amusement of this sort we embarked again and went right out to sea amid the thunder of the forts that guard the mouth of the river. There was not much to see on this excursion, but in the evening we were rowed about the water to look at the illuminations, which were most effective, the whole town from the river being outlined in fire, as well as all the rigging of the ships. We also visited a house on the water belonging to a notable, who received every one of us with a profound salâm, made in an unusual manner by lowering *both* hands to the ground. Herodotus remarks that when two Egyptians meet in the street they do not speak to each other but salute, " lowering the hand down to the knee."* This description, I make no doubt, refers to the salute as still customary. For the formal Egyptian greeting now consists of two principal actions: first, a sweep of the right hand downwards towards the knee, then a rapid touching of the breast, lips, and forehead. The meaning of it all is said to be, " I take up the dust before you; my heart, lips, and head are at your service." But the full salute would not be exchanged between

---

* Herodotus, book ii. chapter 80.

equals on ordinary occasions, and it is rendered with greater or less emphasis according to the rank of the persons concerned. Equals often omit the preliminary scrape, but go on moving the hand backwards and forwards from lip to chest; there are also hand-shakings and curious alternate thumb-grippings to be interchanged. A mere *passing* salute between equals is generally little more than our military salute.

From Damietta we returned by river to Mansûra, thence, by the Khedive's own train in very sumptuously furnished carriages, to Zagazig. The train stopped at all stations on the way for the Khedive to receive petitions and addresses. Music was always in readiness, and at one place a regular litany was recited by an Imâm, with a chorus who repeated Amin (Amen) at the end of every verse; and every verse was a prayer for the welfare of the Khedive.

Zagazig was the beginning of troubles to us. The suite were put up in the mudiriah or house of the mudir. My first room was a mere cabin, having a mud floor covered by a worn felt carpet, and having two oblong holes in the wall for windows; one window had shutters; neither was glazed, nor had the door any sort of fastening. There was no chair, no table, nothing to wash with. This room was unbearable. I tried a second room and abandoned it, then a third, which proved to be a loft over a fowl-house: so in despair I returned to the second. It had bare rafters and whitewashed walls, a mud floor covered by reed matting, with two Turkey rugs, a shaky door, a stone divan with cushions, a tiny table on which stood a bottle of water in a plate. Fortunately I had brought a great ewer and basin of native ware, or one might have gone unwashen. We dined at the house of Amín Bey, a rich landed proprietor. It was dinner *à la Turque;* but in the open air, under vine-trellises and surrounded by roses, one could endure a good deal. Our host waited on us, and noticed the embarrassment of the Europeans.

Next morning I was awakened early by sparrows flying about my room. Sulimân catered for breakfast, and provided a roll, some eggs, a *bakarag* of native coffee, a covered bowl of milk, and one tablespoon. Thus I managed to make a sort of *café-au-lait*, and the only egg which was not rotten was eaten with the table-spoon. After breakfast I rode to the ruins of Bubastis,* but found nothing except vast rubbish-mounds with here and there a fragment of a column.

---

* See Herodotus, book ii. chapters 60, 138.

Fine antiques are, however, unearthed occasionally, as I shall instance later on. It was the English telegraphist here who first heard from the sheikhs and pilgrims from Mecca of the gold in Midian, and also prompted Captain Burton to undertake the expedition thither.

The tediousness of another day at Zagazig was relieved by a curious and barbaric procession of dervishes, in which figured men eating serpents and glass, half-nude swordsmen, and men clad in tin armour, with helmets and cuirasses like those of the old Mamelukes; but the most conspicuous weapon in the procession was the dabûs—a long spike, with a round wooden head hung about with tiny chains. This spike is used to thrust through the arms or cheeks by very pious dervishes.

Amîn Bey astonished us at luncheon that day; for, instead of the Turkish meal we had expected, we found under our vine-bower a long table covered with a snowy cloth; dishes piled with delicious fruits standing amid pots of splendid flowers, iced champagne and claret, and, above all, plates, knives, and forks to the heart's content. Amîn Bey, with his usual cleverness, had taken the hint of last night, and had made this surprising transformation. He wished to do us honour; only at first he mistook our tastes. I believe since then the great man has fallen with oriental swiftness.

In the evening the Khedive went by special train to visit the country-house of a notable called Sheikh Sulimân 'Agâzah. From the place where the train stopped a road had been formed and lined with lanterns. It ended in a great square marked out by arcades of painted woodwork with brilliantly lighted arches. From the square we passed through beautiful gardens redolent of roses, whose coloured petals glimmered dimly through the scented gloom. Within doors the sheikh entertained us with coffee and syrup served in covered silver cups. It was a short visit of ceremony, and we soon mounted our horses again and were under the stars. Those Egyptian nights were glorious; their remembrance is a perpetual treasure.

On the day of our departure from Zagazig we rose at five o'clock, and reached the station by six. On these mornings there was never any breakfast provided, and at the station we had usually to wait two hours before starting. The weary waiting over, we set off to Tantah, where we were again housed in the awful squalor of the mudir's "palace." Two beds in one small room, floors literally an inch deep in filthy dust, and raging with bugs. At Tantah the Khedive received Sir Rivers Wilson and the Commissioners of Liquidation, and drove them about to see the illuminations. But an illness resulting from the bad food, the venomous odours, the savage insects, and the fiery sirocco wind, has left Tantah a dreary blank in my memory.

For it was now the last week of April, and, though the Khamsin, or Fifty-days Wind, had not begun to blow regularly, we were just getting a foretaste of it. It comes from the south with a roar like a furnace, and bends the palms down nearly to breaking; it clouds the skies with a mist of fine, impalpable sand, and dulls the sun to a pale and sickly hue. All the brightness and the freshness of nature are gone; the world seems lapped by a devouring flame of fire. Every window of the house must be tightly shut, but in vain; the sand and the flame pierce within. Chairs, tables, and mirrors crack with a loud report; water vanishes like magic from the vessels that held it; men sleep, or lie prostrate wishing for sleep; movement is a burden; reading, writing, even thinking, is a misery. This state of things lasts day and night for four or five days, sometimes even ten days together; then it changes, and the northern breezes blowing again give a brief respite. But one has hardly time to revel in the delicious coolness of the sea-wind when the sirocco leaps forth again from the south, and scorches the land with a blast of fire.

At Shibîn el Kôm our accommodation was rather better, and one was at least in the country, where the groves of peach, fig, and above all orange, made cool and shady walks. Not that any other member of the Khedive's suite ever dreamed of taking a country walk: the idea is foreign to the true Egyptian, unless he happens to be a lunatic. There is a story told of an old woman who moved from Windermere to a slum in Manchester. When the curate condoled with her on the change, she remarked, "Sorry to leave those hills? No, indeed. I like a place where there is something to see." But this is not quite analogous to the pasha's frame of mind. He would say, "All places are alike to the true believer. The servant of God is passive, not elective. Doubtless Iblis the accursed beguiles infidels to love walking or travel, but it is written on the pages of the air that sitting is better." How different are these people from the Egyptian lords of the middle ages, the battle-loving, polo-playing Saracens.

The drinking-fountains in this region are curious

and picturesque. By the wayside here and there may be seen tiny domed structures, about six feet square on plan. Each incloses a large earthen vessel which is built round with solid masonry a yard high, and above the vessel rises a cupola supported on four open arches. A kûllah or drinking-bottle rests on the flat surface beside the edge of the water-jar. These little wayside fountains are maintained and kept in repair by the mosques.

A rather novel entertainment was provided here by a Greek merchant, who had a fine dahabiah on the canal. While both banks of the canal were lit with lamps and fireworks, the dahabiah moved slowly along the dark water, its deck, upper deck, sails, and rigging, all outlined with lanterns. The effect was brilliant and unusual: generally these illuminations were feeble and wearisome in sameness.

The tents too of the sheikhs assembled at Shibîn were of great magnificence; they were adorned inside with the *appliqué* work common in the country, the designs consisting of flowers, fruits, animals, conventional symbols, and verses of the Korân arranged with wonderful taste and symmetry. One tent is said to have cost 2000*l*. The Khedive's tent of French silk with silver-mounted poles was no doubt costly, but much less beautiful.

Besides the Greek merchant, Shibin was famous for an ancient saint called Sirsinnah el Shûhada, and for a notable called 'Ali Bey Shaiur. The Khedive visited the saint's tomb under a large escort of Beduins; and in the evening 'Ali Bey entertained at dinner the principal members of the suite—Talat Pasha, Khairi Pasha, Zeki Pasha, Rashid Pasha, Mustafa Pasha, and Goudard Bey; I alone plain Mister among all the unspeakable grandees. Our host lived in a fine large house furnished in European style; but the dinner was entirely native. A slave was standing at the entrance to the dining-room holding a silver ewer, from which he poured water on the hands of every guest as he entered, and caught the water in a silver basin. Each guest had a fine gold-embroidered napkin to dry his hands. We had no plates, knives, forks, or glasses; but one spoon apiece. The table was, as usual, a large circular tray set on a pedestal. For drink, a slave was in waiting with a single tumbler with which he supplied the muddy water of the place, as called upon. Each course consisted of one dish set in the centre of the table, and the guests helped themselves. The courses were: 1, soup. All dipped their spoons into the bowl and kept so dipping them. 2, A whole sheep roasted; this they tore with their fingers, rifling the bones, and digging about for choice morsels of meat. 3, Artichokes in oil. 4, Rolls of pastry. 5, Stewed fowl. 6, Bamias—a kind of vegetable. 7, An indescribable native sweetmeat. Rashîd Pasha broke off a morsel, and set it before me; this was an honour. 8, Rice pudding. 9, A cake adorned with silvered sweets. 10, Pilâf, a savoury preparation of rice. 11, Pigeons with green peas floating in oil. Zeki Pasha took a pigeon by the leg, and smiling, placed it on my bread; this was an honour. 12, Chickens. 13, Knuckle-bones. 14, Another sort of pilâf. 15, A salmi of something. 16, Another sort of cake. 17, More meat. 18, Almond biscuits. 19, Sweet syrup, flavoured with rose-leaves. 20, Watermelons and strawberries. Altogether a most prodigious meal. When it was over we washed our hands again, —there were some who needed it—and retired to another room for coffee and smoking.

Presently our host, who had been dining with the Khedive, entered, bowing low and salâming with many apologies to the whole company. With great condescension the pashas invited him to be seated. Taking a seat is always the signal for the whole company to exchange greetings with the new-comer.

The greeting over, our host sat nervously balanced on the edge of his chair, his coat-tails drawn meekly forward over his knees, his hands folded in an attitude of deep humility, his eyes reverently downcast. For about ten minutes nobody spoke to him or noticed him further. Then a pasha cordially pressed him to take one of his own cigarettes; he ventured to comply in some trepidation. Silence again. Then they praised his rafters and rooms, to his great confusion. The poor man was dreadfully uncomfortable, and only relieved when an hour after dinner we departed. Horses were in waiting to take us to our quarters and torch-bearers as a guard of honour.

Next day we left for Damanhûr, and of course a travelling day was breakfastless; but I managed to get a stale roll and some muddy water before starting. During the last few miles of our journey a number of Beduins raced with the train. Several times as they tore along at mad speed a horse fell, and those in the press behind, unable to stop, rolled over, horses and riders together, in a way that made one shudder. They seemed utterly reckless, but it was impossible to see whether any were killed or seriously hurt, as the train passed on.

Walking through the bazaars here I heard a man

coming from behind and shouting continually some phrase about the Prophet. He forced his way along, and in passing elbowed me aside in a cool, careless way that was very provoking. With an angry exclamation I sent him flinging. When he recovered he levelled a glance of fury at me, but after a pause resumed his way, crying aloud as before. Subsequently I found that he was a madman, and that his cry was, "Whoso loves the Prophet, let him pray!" I was sorry, therefore, for having resented his behaviour, but glad that no worse result followed.

For a great part of the day here the Khedive sat in his tent. Petitions of all sorts kept pouring in, but it was evident that the poor people had not much faith in their petitions being answered unless they could deliver them to the Khedive personally. A crowd stood at a distance before the tent all day, and often a man or woman would on a sudden dart out of the throng across the open space and make a rush for the Khedive's presence; but sentries always interfered and took away the petition for a more formal delivery. One poor fellow gave great trouble, and when at last he understood that his paper would be duly presented, he sat for hours with eyes riveted on the Khedive's tent, his face wearing a look of most pathetic anxiety. All petitions, as a matter of fact, were answered, though most treated of no high and mighty matter. Thus one man complained that, having mortgaged his house for 10*l*., he was unable to redeem it. The Khedive gave him the money. Another said his donkey had been stolen. A poor woman begged the release from prison of her brother in the Faiûm. Not only petitioners, but beggars of many kinds and cripples, stood at a distance from the tent asking for alms, and all got something.

At a *café* to-day I saw a boy hawking enormous lettuces, which the frequenters bought; but they threw away the leaves and eat the stalk—a reversal of European custom not noticed by Herodotus. I saw, also, a woman wade into the canal with a large market-basket on her head; though the water was above her waist, she walked on afterwards in the most nonchalant manner, without even stooping to wring her clothes. Another sight here that amused me was the appearance of one of the suite in the deepest mourning; he had not lost a relation, but had received a reproof from the Khedive.

From Damanhûr we moved to Dasûk, where the customary ox was sacrificed, and where the only enlivenment was a combat that raged over the brute's remains. One party of ten men had together seized the raw hide, and, while all ran riverwards, were fighting five a side for its possession. They disappeared in a body through the door of a house. Next came four men who had secured a fine piece of the ribs. They ran down to the shore, hotly pursued; rolled their meat swiftly down the steep, dusty bank to the water's edge, caught it up, and flung it and themselves into a boat. Then with their oars they beat off their pursuers, and pushed with merry hearts across the river.

The Mudir of Dasûk has a fine house, in the hall of which I dined with the pashas strictly *à la Turque*. Later the Khedive came to pay a visit of ceremony; and just as he was mounting the marble steps a huge scarab appeared on the carpet spread for his feet; and the emblem of ancient Egypt was hustled away with scant honour before the Lord Pharaoh of to-day.

It was on May-day that we reached the beautiful town of Rosetta. Nothing can exceed the charm of its ancient palaces and colonnaded streets; nor is the venerable desolation of its buildings more striking than the perennial freshness of its gardens. The houses here are huge structures in three or four stories, built almost entirely of brick; but the surface

ANCIENT HOUSE AT ROSETTA.

of the walls is relieved by a sort of mosaic brickwork, in which varied designs are set in harmonious colours. The upper stories project, and the corbels upholding them often rest upon marble pillars of Greek or Roman work. In the best houses the windows are covered with exquisite mushrabiah or lattice-work set with tiny oriels; and within doors abound splendidly carved and painted ceilings of woodwork, and dadoes and pavements of marble mosaic. What strikes one here above all is the unchanged mediævalism of the ancient city. Its very decay has saved it; there has been no call here for restorer or improver. Rosetta is still the Rosetta of the sixteenth century not of the nineteenth; and the remains of Arab or rather Coptic art here are unrivalled.

A walk to the southern fort gives one a lovely view of the winding Nile, the palmy desert, and the rich gardens, as well as of the antique city. Near the fort, however, one passes over an uncanny-looking spot—a space of adder-haunted sand, seamed with serpents' tracks, full of holes, dwellings of the dreaded sand-viper, which buries itself and strikes the passer-by unawares. One sees also on the sand many strange marks of little paws, which are probably chameleon traces.

As at Damietta, we ran down to the sea in our steamers. We passed Fort St. Julien, where the famous Rosetta stone was found. It is a small old brick building with thick walls half in ruins. The banks of the Nile here are low and covered with forests of palms, each tree of which pays, or then paid, a tax of sixteen shillings a year to the Government. We landed on the western promontory, with the Khedive, and all were much amused by a fat pasha jumping plump into a quicksand. When we had embarked again we continued down-stream till we reached the open sea. The sea-breezes were to some of us delightful, to others detestable.

I was talking to a good-natured Arab on board, and looking over the waves I remarked, "I am glad to see English territory again," meaning, of course, the sea. "You mean Egypt, I suppose?" he exclaimed, and laughed. "No," I said, "I have seen Egypt every day for three months past; I mean the sea." The manner in which he caught up my remark at least showed his ruling idea. Yesterday the same man said to me, "Egypt is like a big rich bone guarded by two powerful dogs, England and France. While the huge dogs glare and growl at each other, the ants crawl all over the bone, plunder it and get fat. The ants are Greeks, Italians, and Levantines." I thought the comparison clever, and at the time it was certainly true. Since then there has been a wild alarm, one of the big dogs retreated with his tail between his legs, the other after a brisk but easy fight has retired with the bone to a manger.

Our expedition was accompanied by a native photographer, who had very little skill and no idea of choosing a subject. At Rosetta I took him in hand, and after a great deal of trouble got him to take one or two fine old houses. About eight months afterwards the proofs were actually ready and turned out satisfactory. Rosetta, fortunately, is so far removed from the main lines of traffic that Europeans rarely visit it, and it has some chance of saving its precious relics of mediæval art. But Europeans are not the only destroyers: the Arab is nearly as bad as the Frenchman. It was only the other day that these Rosetta houses were being pulled down for the value of the bricks. So cheap were the desolate tenements that it paid to destroy them and to transport the materials to Alexandria for building. But this is now forbidden.

We left Rosetta on the 3rd of May,—a day called Shem-en-Nesim, or "Smell the Zephyr": it is a sort of May-day, originally a Coptic festival, but now adopted also by the Muslims. We started before dawn, and at seven o'clock landed to walk in some lovely palace gardens on the banks of the river. There we smelt our zephyr and gathered roses; for this is the feast of flowers. Later on in the day we passed boats full of people piping, singing, dancing, and clapping their hands exactly in the manner described of old by Herodotus.* Their method of clapping hands is not like that of Europeans. It is a slow measured beat, in which the palms are struck together *vertically* in front of the chest; and it is done by all together in time. We passed also the dead body of a fellah floating down the stream; many persons were on the bank close by; but no one regarded it. The man was dead; accident, suicide, murder,—what did it matter?

A long journey next day brought us back to Cairo, which we reached soon after sunset, and landed amid thunder of cannon from the Citadel. So I had travelled along both branches of the Nile from the First Cataract to the sea—a route few travellers ever care to accomplish.

* Herodotus, book ii. chapter 60.

CHAPTER IV.

Mr. Gladstone and Turkey — An unjust steward — The devil's muezzin — Colonel Gordon and the Khedive — First signs of the Rebellion — Stories of fortunes — The pyramids in summer — Great procession of dervishes.

THE day after our return I dined with the Khedive — present: Talat, Khairi, Yûsuf, Zeki, and Sâlim Pashas, also Shauki and Tonino Beys. The Khedive spoke to me the whole evening in English; Sâlim was the only one who could follow the conversation. A *levée* had been held that day at which His Highness received fully eight hundred people; he was tired, but, as usual, very animated. After some remarks and questions about our journey through the Delta, he began to speak of English politics. The elections had just returned Mr. Gladstone to power with a crushing majority, but the Khedive was under the idea that the Queen had no affection for her new

Premier. On the other hand, the Russians, he added according to the information of his agents at Stambûl, were delighted by the accession of Mr. Gladstone, the enemy of Turkey and the friend of Russia. The Khedive, however, was much impressd by the national union of England, despite party differences; the idea of a great people with one mind drew forth his warmest expressions of admiration. He noticed, also, that English people abroad uncover to a foreign sovereign, whereas people of other nations do not, or do so rarely. He praised English liberty with great heartiness, agreeing readily to my remark that there was far more individual freedom in monarchical England than in republican France. In the drawing-room after dinner our conversation reverted to Lower Egypt. His Highness admired Damietta more than all the other places we had visited, but in this I could not agree. Damietta had more commerce, and possibly a finer situation, but in point of art and architecture I thought Rosetta far more beautiful. So we talked on, and on taking leave I went as usual to sit in the palace gardens with the suite. From them I heard now and then curious anecdotes.

Thus there was and is in the service of the Khedive a certain man whom I will only call the negro, for such he is. In old times this man had some influence with the ex-Khedive Ismail, an influence which he turned to excellent profit. In our late journey, the cunning Ethiopian had been trading on his position in the same way, pretending that he was still a great person. Here is a dialogue overheard between the negro and a village sheikh—

"The cows you sent last time were not as good as I could wish; have you no better?"

"Certainly, Excellency: it was a bad season last year, so it was written: but please God now the beasts are fatter."

"Good; and have you any poultry?"

"I have, Excellency."

"Very well; send me some poultry."

"I hear and obey."

"And, my dear friend, have you any butter?"

"My butter is your butter."

"And you will not forget the dates, when the clusters are gathered."

"On the head and the eye; your slave is much honoured."

"You are a honest man, by the beard of the Prophet; and I will speak well of you before Effendina. Peace be with you."

"With you be peace; may God whiten your face."

They part. The poor sheikh has some misgiving, but obeys in fruitless hope; the nigger pockets his gains, and thoroughly enjoys the transaction. Verily his was a neck to be beaten with shoes.

Another evening, after having dined with the Khedive, I had a chat in the gardens about General, or, as he then was, Colonel Gordon. All agreed in saying, oddly enough, that he was a very bad administrator, though a splendid soldier. Sálim Pasha said that Gordon ruined scores of people by his capricious and causeless changes from friendship to enmity; and that it would take years to repair the mischief which he had done in the Sudân. All the people about the Court entertained this curious opinion, which I recall without further comment, beyond suggesting jealousy as the motive of their censure. But at this time Gordon had resigned his governorship of the Sudân, and was no longer in Egypt.

Cairo was now startled by a rumour that a caravan of slaves had reached Siût. Most people said it was impossible; nevertheless it was true. The caravan had travelled forty days across the desert with untold suffering to the miserable slaves: but by taking the long desert route they had reached Egypt without being discovered by the authorities. By the then existing law slaves could be bought and sold privately from house to house with their own consent, *i. e.*, provided they made no complaint to the Government. They were often paid, and preferred slavery to freedom. A slave-girl could claim freedom if she wished to get married. But it was settled that in 1885 even the system of private purchase should for ever cease.

Ismail had a way of palming off his slaves on his courtiers. In this manner he once sent for my friend F——, the tall handsome-looking officer of the Ceremonies,—a man in fact whom a native would call "the crushing lion and the splendid moon"—and said, "I have found you a wife like a Huriah of Paradise; you will marry her in a fortnight." "Your Highness," he replied, "does me too much honour. I am overwhelmed with happiness." The marriage duly took place, and of course F—— never saw his bride until the rites were over. Then, when at last the veil was removed, the bridegroom found himself wedded to an unspeakably hideous negress. One sight was enough; he fled, and never went near her again; but on Ismail's downfall and departure he divorced her, and married a wife to his mind.

The slave-trade does and must continue as long as the demand continues. If slave-trade abolition societies would devote their funds to social reform and education in the East, they would be striking at the root of the slave-trade. The palliatives at which they now aim are at best moderately and temporarily successful, and in some cases even cause aggravated suffering and brutality. The evil can only be cured by removal of the causes, not by trying to suppress the symptoms. But in Cairo slaves as a rule are happy enough. I dined one day with an Englishman, who, pointing to a Sudâni waiting at table, said,—

"There's one of the results of the abolition of the slave-trade in Egypt."

"You rescued him?"

"No, I bought him. The trade of course continues."

"But you pay him, I suppose?"

"No," replied my host, "what is the use? At one time I used to give him money, but he never knew what to do with it."

"But, if he chooses, he can claim his liberty, can he not?"

"Yes, and what then? he would starve. Nobody dare take a runaway slave for fear of the master's enmity. I have dismissed him two or three times already; he always came back, and begged on his knees to be received again into slavery."

We were now in the middle of the abominable khamsîn wind, during which I occasionally sought a vain refuge from the heat in a dahabiah moored upon the Nile; but there was no peace beneath those yellow insufferable skies. Travellers, of course, had all departed, and there was scarcely an Englishman left in Cairo. The two or three remaining met occasionally at the consulate for lawn-tennis, or rather sand-tennis; for the court was made of sand mixed with earth and rolled. I found that one could play a brisk game of tennis when it was so hot that to stand still in the sun was dangerous. By wearing a turban and retiring into the shade directly the game was over, one might play with safety under the fiercest sun. My racquet was at first a great puzzle to the Arabs at the palace; but they succeeded in explaining it away as a musical instrument, though, doubtless, a most uncanny example of "the devil's muezzin."*

I now became a frequent guest at the Khedive's table, and began to learn something of the pashas'

---

* The name given by the Prophet to any instrument of music, his idea being that music is a call to the service of Satan.

ideas on subjects of morals and politics. The Turks were thoroughly alarmed by the accession of the Liberals to power, as they thought it meant the abandonment of Constantinople to Russia. The Egyptian Turk, however, consoled himself with the reflection that the Liberals, not caring to meddle with foreign politics, would be certain to let Egypt alone.

Nescia mens hominum fati sortisque futurae!

How soon and how sadly came the undeceiving.

But in all these matters I found the Khedive infinitely more enlightened and intelligent than his courtiers. The latter hated and abused England for betraying Turkey in the late war: they were firmly persuaded that Turkey made war by the advice of England under promise of English help, and was deserted by English treachery. They were very jealous of English influence in Egypt, jealous of the Khedive talking and learning English, jealous even of me. I knew very well that, for all their smooth and honeyed words to me, nearly every man's hand was against me, and that webs of intrigue were woven in every corner of the palace to catch unwary words or actions. But this knowledge only enlarged the interest of my position.

Four months had now passed since my arrival in

Egypt, and I began to wonder whether I should ever do any work with my pupils; when one fine day the Khedive sent for me and said,—"The princes will begin their lessons to-morrow; they are very young and the heat is great; fifteen minutes a day will be sufficient." So next morning I was introduced to the little princes by their Circassian companion, the genial 'Ali Bey. Let me say at once that more charming children it is impossible to imagine. The eldest, 'Abbas Bey, was then six years old, and Mohammed 'Ali, the younger, was barely five. They were, of course, as fair as most Europeans; had bright, pretty faces, and most winning manners. 'Abbas Bey was remarkable for his sweetness of disposition; Mohammed 'Ali for a roguishness, that soon made me christen him "Little Mischief." Both had good abilities, and it was a real pleasure to teach them.

But one thing troubled me. The Circassian's presence during the lesson was desireable, and not irksome. But I did not at all like the presence of two black servants, who stood by watching every movement and ignorantly gaping at every word. The first day I said nothing; but, when the blacks on the second day pried and stared in their foolish gaby manner, I could stand it no longer, and said sharply in Arabic,

"Have the goodness to remain outside." The order was received with some astonishment, but promptly obeyed. In the evening I told the Khedive, who approved what I had done, and commanded that no servant should for the future be present.

Apart from the added pleasure of teaching my delightful little pupils, life now became very full and interesting. I had means of knowing nearly all that was going on, and understood more of the secret hopes and fears then ruling the Court than the good pashas imagined. One night they had a long discussion on the probable future of Egypt on the downfall of Turkey, which all anticipated. I was not present, but I could name those who maintained that the annexation of Egypt by England was inevitable, and those who held that Egypt, even if separated from Turkey, could be neutralised, like Belgium, under the guarantee of Europe. Now when decision between these two alternatives is the burning question of the hour, it is curious to see how clearly the case was realised in Egypt in 1880.

The arrival of the slave-caravan at Siût had made a great disturbance. No one was more sincerely annoyed by it than the Khedive, whose unfeigned hatred of the slave-trade impressed me the more deeply the longer I knew him. Count Sala was at once appointed with a roving commission for the suppression of the traffic in Egypt; his headquarters were to be Siût; and he had a troop of five hundred horse placed at his disposal. The natives wanted a native chief of the commission; but a native would only have turned the office to profit by taking bribes to allow the practice which he was ordered and paid to prevent. That is the beaten road to riches in Egypt.

The scandal of the slave-caravan at Siût ended after all rather tamely; for ninety out of the one hundred slaves were brought to Cairo and released. The fact is that the slave-dealers, finding that they could not secure a profitable market for their slaves, turned informers against themselves, and so got rewarded. Smugglers on the coast have a somewhat similar method; if they find it difficult to run a cargo of tobacco, they employ confederates to inform the revenue officers. The tobacco is promptly seized, the confederates are handsomely rewarded, and the confederates also are generally able to purchase the confiscated cargo at a price far below its market value. Thus they get their double profit.

On the 20th of May Lord Ripon landed at Alexandria, on his way to India, bringing with him Colonel Gordon as his private secretary. Gordon, it seems, had heard through the newspapers of the slave-caravan at Siût, and accordingly he wrote from Alexandria to the Khedive a letter, in which he said: "I do not like you, and the people of England do not like you. The English people like the Sultan of Zanzibar and the King of Abyssinia better than you, because you encourage the slave-trade." This letter, of course, was very unjust. But on his way through Egypt to Suez Gordon learnt the facts of the case—that the Khedive had dismissed the governor of Siût, had appointed Count Sala with full powers to repress the slave-trade, and himself by every means discouraged it. Upon this Gordon wrote again from Suez, saying: "I was wrong yesterday in what I wrote to you. I now know what you have done, and I like you very well." The officials in Egypt generally regarded Gordon as *un peu troublé*—his character was beyond their understanding.

Four days after the departure of Gordon arose the first murmurs of the storm which since has shaken Egypt. Rumours got abroad of a conspiracy to massacre all the Christians in Cairo, and Mr. Malet, the English consul, brought these rumours to the Khedive's notice. There was this much truth in the story. Some half-pay men and others in the army sent a threatening letter to the Minister of War, alleging that they were kept on full duty though on half pay; that their arrears and pensions were not discharged; that a distinction was drawn between natives and Europeans, the latter receiving fair treatment and regular payment; and, finally, that if these complaints were disregarded the army would have recourse to the sword. For the moment nothing came of this letter. Its sequel was the bombardment of Alexandria, the capture of Cairo by the English, the betrayal of Khartûm and death of Gordon, and—but the drama is not yet finished.

I noticed sentries and patrols about the streets as I walked home from Ismailia Palace to 'Abdîn that night, and the next evening, too, as I returned from dining out with Mr. L——; but the matter was soon forgotten. Mr. L—— is a splendid old Indian, full of Mutiny and tiger stories. I met at his house an official, now engaged in investigating the payment of land-tax. He told me that he had discovered several rich landowners who for years past had paid nothing, and that in such cases he recovered four years' payment—all that is allowed by the Egyptian statute of limitations, even under claim of the crown. Thus the mudir of Tantah had just paid up 900*l.* It is a common practice for a wealthy man who covets the land of a poor neighbour to force the latter into signing a deed of transfer, and to seize the land, yet, by a refinement of iniquity, to leave the dispossessed fellah to pay the taxes. Many of these mudirs and others exercise the kûrbash, or bastinado, with the most brutal severity. Formally it is abolished; practically it is necessary in some degree; secretly it is abused horribly.

On the Queen's birthday the Khedive sent a congratulatory telegram, to which the Queen replied, conveying her thanks in the first person, not through an officer of the household. The Khedive was much flattered at this mark of kindness, and all the Court felt themselves highly honoured.

One hears so many stories in Egypt that one is cautious of believing any. Let me give a story of a fortune as it was related to me. The great banking-house of ———— are said to have started as follows in Egypt. A certain small banker of the name received a visit from a client, a very rich pasha, who was on the point of making a journey to Constantinople, and intended to reside there during the summer. The pasha would require money from time to time: would —— advance it? "Certainly," was the reply, "but to avoid trouble you had better leave me a number of blank drafts bearing your signature; as you require money, telegraph, I will fill them up, and you can draw at Constantinople." All went well for some weeks, the money was duly paid, and the bills made out, till suddenly there came a telegram to the banker from his agent in Constantinople, saying "The pasha is dead." The banker at once filled up the remaining drafts for very large sums, got the signature duly attested, and ultimately recovered the money out of the pasha's estate, of which little was left for the heir.

Here is another story of triumphant robbery. At Alexandria lives a certain official belonging to a European state, who began life not as an official nor even as a European, but as a small Levantine money-lender. He now possesses untold wealth, which he acquired in this manner. Under the former Khedive Ismail the possession of great riches was extremely dangerous to the possessor. So a certain pasha, fearing for his immense estates, went to ——, and made an agreement by which —— should have and keep for public purposes a deed of gift, transferring the whole property to himself; at the same time the money-lender gave the pasha a document, dated subsequently, which rendered the deed of transfer null and void. The latter arrangement was designed to guard the pasha against trickery, but was of course kept a profound secret. In consideration of the security thus obtained for his estates, the pasha agreed to pay —— a regular percentage on his income, while continuing to administer the property as before. One night, not long afterwards, the pasha died very suddenly—as rich men often do in the East. So tender are their digestions that a cup of coffee is often fatal. On hearing the news, the money-lender rushed off to the pasha's palace, contrived to possess himself of the secret document, knowing exactly where it was kept, and promptly burnt it. He then flourished the deed of gift in the face of the pasha's family, established his claim before the tribunals, and for his wealth, ability, and virtue, received a handsome appointment and a patent of nobility from a European potentate.

Some amusement was caused at the Court one day by a letter written from England by a poor lunatic to the Khedive. The writer at one time called himself the Holy Ghost, at another King of England, and informed the Khedive that he was coming to claim dominion over Egypt, Africa, India, and all the countries of the East. Some of the courtiers were actually alarmed, and took the thing quite *au sérieux*. But they were very nervous on all foreign questions. For some time past they had been haunted by fears of a war with Abyssinia, but were much relieved to hear that the Queen had written a letter to King John, and that on receiving it the King had declared that he would never again think of quarrelling with Egypt.

The Khedive, however, was much exercised by a severe article in *The Times* on the revival of the slave-trade. I must say, in fairness, that the article was quite inaccurate in its facts, and consequently unjust in its conclusions. Tewfik was really and heartily striving for the abolition of slavery, though his task was difficult. Most of the people in Egypt, and of the pashas about the Court, were in arms against the reform; I alone lost no opportunity of encouraging His Highness, though the want of appreciation shown him in England was enough to dishearten the most zealous.

Dining with the Khedive I had an interesting conversation about the Egyptian army and navy; then about the news from Constantinople, where Mr. Goschen was on a mission. The Khedive had just received a letter stating that the Sultan sent his Master of Ceremonies every day to Mr. Goschen, asking him to modify certain public utterances, which had given great offence at Stambûl. His Highness next spoke of the banishment of Shâin Pasha, who left Egypt that day never to return. He was originally a seller of cakes in the streets; but in true Arabian Nights fashion got into favour with Khalîf Ismail, and in his service amassed a fortune of 100,000*l.*, besides large landed estates. He was now exiled for intriguing against his sovereign. Speaking of another banished pasha, the Khedive told me that Naib had possessed no less than seven hundred slaves; that from the account-books which Naib left behind on his flight it appears that he was in the habit of continually bribing the railway officials at Bûlak-ed-Dakrûr, giving 200*l.* here, 400*l.* there, and so on, to secure their connivance at the transport of slaves to Cairo for his own household. A batch of one hundred girls came at a single consignment for Naib, and were first concealed in detachments with various old women, and then quietly transferred to the pasha's abode.

This story Tewfik related from his own knowledge. Naib once gave 25,000*l.* for a single Circassian beauty. Yet this is the man who made England and Europe believe that he wished to abolish the slave-trade. The fact is that he wished to figure as a man of enlightenment and a reformer, and acted the part admirably on the stage: behind the scenes he was a tyrannical slave-hunter.

As the conversation now fell upon the taxes paid by the fellahin, I ventured to tell the Khedive that some of the sheikhs or mudirs were in the habit of seizing land, and forcing the owners to sign it away. He admitted that such things had happened even quite recently, but added that the practice was now stopped under the new system, which had relieved the fellahin also of many oppressive taxes, and, above all, fixed in black and white the amount of each man's contribution; thus securing him against the extortion of the agents and collectors who farmed the taxes before. The Khedive told me of a certain miserable Englishman, who had turned Musulman, and was then living not far from Cairo in the enjoyment of considerable property, which he had been careful to acquire with the four silly wives who had married him. The rascal had avoided payment of all taxes, until the inspector came down upon him, and demanded 2000*l*. as arrears under penalty of confiscating his land. Of course the money was paid. The name of the creature I could tell, but suppress intentionally.

All this conversation was carried on in English, and was understood by no one except Turâbi and myself. When any name occurred which would have betrayed the subject, the Khedive spelt it, or gave the first two letters; so the pashas were not much the wiser. They sat in glum silence, and I fear the thoughts of their hearts to me were not tender. A day or two later there was another great debate in the palace gardens about the future of Egypt. Turâbi said that if the Turkish empire were to fall,—" which God forbid,"—England would be forced to take Egypt, as it is the key of the highway to India. Sâlim Pasha was furious at the idea. Tonino mildly deprecated it, and the *valet de chambre*, the rich man and the great, violently abused the notion. This debate, like all conversations, was reported to the Khedive—with amendments. Thus poor Turâbi was represented as having prayed for the speedy downfall of Turkey and the occupation of Cairo by the British! The Khedive at dinner taxed Turâbi with having uttered these sentiments. Turâbi indignantly denied it, told the true story, and said before all the others: "Your Highness sees from this abominable falsehood what the people are who surround you; it was they whose lying intrigues ruined your father, and they are just the same now, always lying and intriguing." All the pashas looked hard at their plates, amazed at the energy of Turâbi's language. The latter continued: "I am Your Highness's devoted servant, and I would lay down my life for you; but I will not be slandered thus. If you believe these people, I am worse than useless to you, and I will take my leave of your service." The Khedive replied simply, "I do not believe them."

There was a terrible buzzing just now in the hive of pashas at the entrance of a certain waspish project for stealing their honey. A Mr. ——— was daily besieging the authorities to sell, or grant a long lease of, the Daira Saniah lands; an English company proposed to take them and farm them, paying a fixed yearly rental considerably larger than the estates could possibly produce under native management. All the pashas were frantic at the idea, citing the case of the conquest of India by a company; the French, headed by their consul-general, were straining every nerve to thwart the project, while on the English side Major Baring and Mr. Malet were urging the Khedive very strongly to sanction it. Promptly there appeared in a leading London paper a statement, that "diplomatic pressure of a rather startling character" had been applied to the Khedive in favour of the company; which statement another leading paper contradicted with official flatness. I have given the truth; but the scheme failed.

The 18th of June, the Khedive's birthday, was celebrated by a *levée* at 'Abdîn. I spent two hours in the anterooms watching the people—some of them very queer people—arrive. Natives, Europeans, Levantines, and Asiatics—how they smoked! When all the visitors had been presented, the courtiers mounted to the state-room, passed in single file before the Khedive, and in passing bowed and saluted.

A few days later I went to the pyramids of Gîzah, anxious to see how they looked in the glory of an Egyptian midsummer. On the way I noticed that the broad plain, which in winter lay covered with green clover and corn, now was black and naked, the thirsty soil baked and gaping with huge cracks, waiting to drink in the Nile, which was fast rising. In the villages men were busily occupied threshing and winnowing their grain in primeval fashion. The threshing is done by two oxen dragging a kind of rude cart in a circle over the corn; the grain is thus loosened, and is winnowed by being tossed in the air, so that the wind may carry off the chaff, which falls in heaps at a little distance.

My companion was a clever and gentlemanly Greek. I had proposed that we should climb the large pyramid, see the sunset, and there dine. So after a visit to the Sphinx and the causeway, then being excavated, we reached the top of the pyramid by seven o'clock. The sun was now very near the horizon, but the moon already had risen high in the east. As the sun vanished, the play of colour was magnificent. Under the moon the eastern horizon was quite dark, sky and plain mingling; just above the darkness was a broad girdle of deep amethystine light, and over that another belt of empurpled crimson; then the full moon, and overhead a dim blue canopy; while on the western horizon was a glow of ruddy gold, which slowly deepened till it faded away. No words can give the right notion of these colours, which are only seen in Egypt and in the summer. Of course there was not a speck of cloud in the sky; no vapour or mist ever was seen at that season, morning or night. Six weeks without sign of a cloud I remember; nor did I ever weary of those cloudless heavens.

While we were in raptures over the sunset our five Arabs were preparing dinner, which was freshened by a huge block of ice, a thing the Arabs professed never to have seen there before. When our salt happened to be blown away by the wind, one of the Beduins offered to run down and get more. He thought less of the descent than an English servant would of running down stairs. After dinner we lay on our backs smoking, star-gazing, and talking with the Arabs. Their talk at times was rather a nuisance. As one was pondering on the awful silence of the scene, surveying the wide horizon, the skies, and the moonlit desert, thinking how grand the pyramid of Chefren looked to-night, with one side deep in shadow, the other silvered with bright light, or recalling, perhaps, quaint Herodotean gossip about the building and builders of the pyramid, it was harsh and jarring to hear an Arab voice strike up,

> " Higgery diggery dugk,
> De mousenup de clugk,
> De clugk street one,
> And den come down run up!"

the echo of a rhyme taught by some crazy traveller.

Such chatter soon put an end to our would-be sublime imaginings. Nevertheless, when we came away, we were agreed that the pyramids are best seen under a midsummer moonlight.

On the way home my Greek, who was an Athenian and a scholar, told me a curious legend of the classical τέττιξ, or cicala. The cicala takes to himself six or seven wives; each wife bores a little hole in the ground and there ensconces herself, leaving only the head projecting. She then lays her eggs. When all the wives have well and truly laid, their lord walks round and bites off the head of each; the body remains, filling the hole, and serves as food to the young offspring as soon as they are hatched. This romance is at least believed by the Athenians.

A great function took place on the 26th, the anniversary of the Khedive's accession. At seven o'clock a.m. a reception was held at 'Abdîn, and soon after there began a grand procession of dervishes, which lasted more than two hours. To the number of quite ten thousand they passed under the windows of the palace, the Khedive watching them from above. Each company had its banners, its music, and its sheikh. The banners were huge, many-coloured, blazoned with texts of the Korân, the music chiefly tom-toms and tambourines, but also brass instruments, flutes, drums, and cymbals. The sheikhs were all mounted on finely-caparisoned horses or donkeys and were attended each by six henchmen. Before each sheikh there came also two men bearing silver thuribles swinging by chains, another man bearing a silver brazier of burning incense, and with him a man bearing a silver salver of incense unkindled; two more men carried silver kumkums, or scent-bottles of liquid perfume, which they scattered about, and behind these came a man with a silver box of dry aromatics. In many cases too the sheikh was preceded by a man carrying his prayer-carpet or by singers chaunting from open books. The singing and music were continuous along the whole line, only here and there resounded antiphons, solemn but monotonous.

Moreover with every company marched a number of men carrying silver-headed staves or maces, and dressed in various uniforms. Thus some wore robes of snowy white with green waistband and green turban; others wore yellow silk robes with black girdles and turbans; a whole tribe wore yellow scarves and yellow turbans. All the colours of the rainbow were there, and a good many others; thus one conspicuous sheikh on horseback was dressed in an orange-coloured outer robe (benish) with kaftân of pale blue silk, a crimson shawl round his shoulders, and a white turban on his head; while behind him on a donkey with scarlet coverlets came his son, clad in white, with a rose-coloured shawl on his shoulders. Some of the sheikhs had sunshades—but very few; and not a man smoked. The procession was varied by odd characters. I saw a sort of fool or jester dressed in scarlet; he wore an enormous shaggy black and green turban, from which long white streamers fell and were laced about his body; he was girt with a scimetar, and brandished a flag in his right hand and a kerchief in his left, as he moved with mincing gait and comic gesture. Another man had merely a tarbûsh or fez on his head, but wore a very thick woollen robe with monkish cowl; he moved at a slow dance instead of walking. Some of the tribes were bareheaded, some wore high conical hats with hair flowing down to the waist; some also were barefoot, while others carried their red or yellow shoes in their hands. Here and there gleamed ancient spears and battle-axes, and everywhere water-carriers with skins or netted pitchers were moving about and clashing their brazen cups together. It was a curious show, and contained Egyptians of all ages, from seven to seventy.

After being received by the Khedive, I drove between lines of saluting sentries down to Ismailia Palace, where I wrote my name in a book, which is the manner of paying respect to Madame la Vice-reine.

UNIV. OF
CALIFORNIA

AN EGYPTIAN VILLAGE IN FLOOD-TIME.

CHAPTER V.

Alexandria – Palace by the sea—Oriental luxury—The *valet de chambre*—A sail—Narrow escape of the Khedive—Fête in the palace gardens—Morice Bey—The sea-shore—Picnic in the desert.

It is customary for the Khedive and Court to pass part of the summer months at Alexandria; and as my rooms at 'Abdin had the sunniest aspect, during the daily and nightly grilling which I received I often longed for the cool sea-breezes.

The summer palace of Râs-el-Tin at Alexandria stands on the promontory of that name—part of the ancient island of Pharos, which has long since been welded to the mainland. The palace is a long, narrow block of buildings running east and west and divided by central corridors. Under its northern windows lie beautiful gardens, shaded by palm and acacia, glowing with flowers of rare scent and splendour, freshened with cool streams and fountains; and beyond the gardens one hears the gentle plash of waves, and looks over the purple waters of the Mediterranean. On the southern side the palace walls are washed by the peaceful billows of the great harbour, which presents an ever-changing picture, as the great ships come and go, or tiny Arab boats scud across its glimmering surface. Altogether a more charming situation cannot be imagined; and the charm once felt can never be forgotten.

The edge was taken off the romance by the first sight of my rooms, or rather room. Two small chambers with a lobby between them were shut off from the corridor. Turâbi occupied one of these, I the other. My room was about ten feet square; it contained nothing but a bed with ragged mosquito-curtains, a divan, a washing-stand, and one chair; no sort of wardrobe or even cupboard, no waterbottle or tumbler, no table; the uneven floor half covered with an old felt carpet, the walls bare unwhitewashed plaster, the ceiling bare deal rafters with glimpses of blue sky between. Yet this rude ventilation probably saved me from a bad illness: the sanitary arrangements were unspeakable. Here then was the reason why my good servant Sulimân had refused to come to Alexandria with me: before I hardly understood his complaints about the palace accommodation. Too bad for a black slave, and was I to endure it? I was furious. I demanded an audience of the Khedive, and got an answer that His Highness was engaged with ministers. This gave me time to cool and reflect. I found that Martino, Tonino, and the other Europeans were as badly off, that there *were* no better rooms except the state apartments, which were magnificent enough, and that the Khedive would doubtless let me go to a hotel in the hot dull European quarter, if I chose to make a fuss. But I soon dismissed the idea of changing the splendid views and fresh sea-breezes of Râs-el-Tin for the stifling atmosphere of the town with a row of white houses for the unvarying prospect. I made up my mind to rough it in the palace, to set off the splendour of seas and skies against the squalor of my lodging.

But not only was I to live in this unhealthy hovel, but for two or three days I got no food to live upon. So Turâbi and I took our meals at a café on the old harbour: it stood on what was probably the site of Anthony's palace, and gave one a splendid view of Fort Pharos, rising boldly from the sea. Our fare was excellent, and we revelled in the breezes. I found that here in Alexandria I was expected to mess with the palace folk, which term included everybody from officers of the ceremonies down to clerks and the *valet de chambre*. This I flatly refused to do. I told the Khedive that I was not accustomed to dine with such people, and that if I could not have my meals alone, as in Cairo, I would continue to take them in the town, at whatever inconvenience. With his usual kindness he gave the requisite order.

I had many proofs that, whatever I suffered, the Khedive was not to blame, and my troubles did not lessen my regard for him. The people about him were incorrigible. Thus I had always to write a list of such things as I required—linen, tea, wine, &c. —and this list I sent in a letter to the bashkâtib or controller of the household. But it often happened that only a part of the things ordered ever reached me, the remainder going as bakshish to somebody, while my letter of demand was taken as a receipt. Once assured of this trickery I wrote in French as follows: " The Tutor to the Sons of the Khedive requires such and such things, and will have the honour of signing his name when he has received them." In reply the list was sent back, copied in Arabic, with a message requiring me to sign it, *i.e.* to give a receipt in advance. To this I sent a peremptory verbal answer by my servant, saying I would not sign until the things were delivered, and if they were not sent I would go straight to the Khedive. This method succeeded; the things came without more ado; and in the end I got my room tolerably furnished.

Let me give another illustration of native character. I have spoken of the *valet de chambre* as a great and powerful personage; I firmly believe that with many of the folk about the Court he ranked next to the Khedive. Frédéric was conjectured to be a Swiss by birth: of which the less said the better. He spoke fairly fluent but very vulgar English, suggestive of low life in London, besides French and Arabic of equal quality. He wore masses of gold, and he flashed with priceless jewels; his clothes were always new and his shoeleather always patent; his wealth was known to be enormous. Because of his wealth, and because he was "near the Khedive," he had great influence; the courtiers were nearly all on equal terms with him, many cringed to him. He would stroll into the ante-room, shake hands all round, smoke loftily, take his coffee haughtily, and in general swagger abominably. When first I used to meet him

I thought him some ill-bred adventurer, and wondered why he claimed my acquaintance. When I found out his position, I effectually put him down, though he required some determined snubbing. The mighty man fell at last from his greatness and retired into private life; but he carried away from Egypt a fortune, with a trifling fraction of which—120,000 francs—he bought a house, and on the vessel by which he returned to Europe he used to brush his hair in the saloon, in order to display his ivory brushes, encrusted with his monogram in diamonds.

There is a curious sort of democracy about an oriental court. Once I was going out driving in the train of the Khedive as was customary, when I saw a certain bey and called to know whether he would join me. After putting my question I noticed that he was with a domestic who serves the Khedive's coffee. The bey, seeing that I was in a carriage large enough to hold four persons, said, "Have you another place to spare?" to which I promptly answered, "No." He got up alone, and as we drove off I said, "Why, that man is a servant, is he not?" "Oh, I don't know," was the answer, "he belongs to His Highness's service." Another afternoon I was walking in the Great Square at Alexandria, holding the inevitable sunshade and smoking a cigar. I met the Court tailor, who, after the custom of the country, shook hands with my companion, while I stood aloof, and, armed with a cigar in one hand and sunshade in the other, declined the proffered honour. That very evening the tailor appeared in the anteroom at the palace, and, nothing daunted, proceeded to shake hands all down the line of beys and pashas who were sitting on divans round the walls. Just before he came to me I leant back on the divan, crossed my legs, and thrust both hands in my pockets. This time my meaning was clear enough: the tailor passed me with a "*Bon jour, monsieur,*" touching his forehead, and from that date he never again offered to shake hands. There were some things in which I would not play the Roman at Rome, but it is not a bad thing with orientals to stand on one's dignity.

The north shore of the Râs-el-Tin promontory was very attractive. Save for two or three sentries, who were generally asleep, not a soul went near it. The pashas, of course, did not care for bathing in quiet pools, climbing about the rocks, or gazing over the melancholy sea. Yet there was always something novel and curious to find—strange shells, anemones, and brilliant-coloured fishes. The most remarkable thing about the rocks was that they contained masses of ancient pottery embedded in their very structure. These fragments were quite unmistakeable, as I examined several very carefully and found on them raised mouldings and line ornamentation decidedly artificial. To me the thing was surprising; it is not so, I believe, to geologists.

Every day on my way to bathe I used to pass a huge Armstrong gun, mounted on a Moncrieff carriage. I often wondered what political combination could ever cause it to be fired in anger, but it proved to be the gun that gave most trouble in this quarter during the bombardment of Alexandria, and I believe it remained uninjured to the end. With regard to the bathing, one felt a certain nervousness of sharks; for the Red Sea shark was said to have found his way through the Canal, as if the smaller tribe native in the Mediterranean were not fierce enough.

My other great pastime was sailing in native craft. The first time I had a mere cockleshell without any ballast, and consequently got a good deal tossed, and a little splashed. I shall never forget the amazement of two pashas, who saw me enter the palace with signs of a sprinkling upon me. "Mâ shâ 'llah, Mâ shâ 'llah, this is terrible; but praise be to God for your safety. There is no power nor might but in God, the High, the Great. The English love the sea; but by my father's beard this is terrible." The boats were rigged with the usual lateen sail, and no doubt in a breeze were somewhat lively: so my excursions were always solitary. A pasha would rather ride the wrong way on his donkey than embark in the stateliest galley upon the calmest sea. Their adage is: *Whoso goeth down to the sea is dead; whoso cometh to land is born alive.* When the Khedive went out and the pashas were free, a few drove about the town, most of them went to the cafés to smoke. They have had only cigarettes at the palace, now they take a nargileh. It is their form of exercise.

But one day the Khedive, who is fond of the sea and fond of a joke, ordered the Court to go for a sail in his yacht at five o'clock. When the order was made known in the afternoon it caused the greatest consternation. Some murmured of destiny and some swore at destiny, while one or two, formed of a more resisting fibre, vowed that nothing should make them go, and retired to their rooms to sleep. But Zeki Bey wrote to each a formal letter from the ante-

K

rooms: "By order of the Khedive you are requested to attend here to receive His Highness's commands at five o'clock." The letter was sent round by an orderly, who carried a book, in which the receiver had to sign an acknowledgment of the order. There was therefore no escape, and all came pale and trembling, or black and lowering.

The yacht is a splendid boat, and makes either a sailing vessel with two masts and two huge lateen sails, or a state galley rowed with twenty oars. The Khedive himself was in a steam-launch with four attendants, ten others of the Court were in the yacht. Among them a good fellow named Wasfi was crazy with terror. Even in the harbour, which is kept always calm by the breakwater, he buried his head in his hands, moaning aloud, and occasionally blurting out a savage remark with a fierce volubility that was very ludicrous. Once, when the boat heeled over a little, his eyes opened large and staring, his face blanched to a ghastly pallor, and he fell down in a fit in the bottom of the boat, where he lay dismally groaning. When he recovered, he slapped his face, crying out, "O, my grief!" and then recited some verses. Outside the harbour, where we got a severe tossing, his terror changed to silent abject despair. Yet we were out a very short time, and he was not the least sea-sick.

Two or three days later, I took the young princes to see an Egyptian frigate anchored in the harbour. The captain received us in state, showed us over the ship, put the men through their gun-drill: then sweetmeats and syrup were served in the state cabin. Quitting the frigate we next visited the two splendid viceroyal yachts, the Masri and the Mahrûssa. The luxury of the fittings was astonishing. The saloon staircase was covered with fine porcelain tiles, the banisters gorgeously inlaid; the columns in all the state-rooms were cased in solid silver, the walls decorated with splendid marquetry, painted panels, gilding, and embroidered silk hangings. Bands played while we looked over the vessels, the guard presented arms as we left and took our seats in the twenty-oared galley, where we reclined on soft cushions of blue velvet embroidered with gold. Cleopatra's barge could scarcely have been more sumptuous.

Another day we had a narrow escape of an accident which would have changed the fortunes of Egypt. I had been out sailing, alone, early in the morning, and had crossed the bay to Fort 'Agameh,—

where subsequently Lord Charles Beresford distinguished himself by his handling of the little Condor. There was a stiff breeze blowing outside the harbour. On my return I was informed that the Khedive would go on the water at five o'clock. He went in the state barge towed by a steam-launch: the ceremonies people and I started ahead on board a sailing-yacht. Our sailors, I saw at once, were a set of ignorant landlubbers who hardly knew stem from stern of the vessel. Our orders were to stand out to sea, passing through a narrow rockbound channel which divides the promontory and the lighthouse fort from the breakwater. I had essayed the same passage in the morning with my tiny craft, and found it impracticable against a head-wind.

Meanwhile the wind and sea had risen; and for a vessel the size of our yacht to attempt the thing was sheer madness. However we had our orders, and went at it. I knew that if once we got in the rough waters of the channel we should infallibly smash against the rocks: so I loosed my coat ready to swim. But fortunately we were beaten off, and failed to make the entrance; the sails flapped, the men swore, and somehow we went about. As we stood away, preparing for a fresh tack, the Khedive's boat suddenly appeared a hundred yards ahead, cutting straight across our course. Our men misreckoned the distance or the speed of the launch, or else were bewildered; and I soon saw that a collision was inevitable. There seemed every prospect of cutting the Khedive's boat through amidships; but at the last moment we altered our course a point or two, instead of putting the helm down and letting the sheet fly; so that we struck at an acute angle instead of a right angle, and with diminished force. Little damage was done, as it happened; but the shock was enough to make one anxious for the Khedive: and I had a rapid vision of making my fortune by a swim, or of being throttled in the water by a fat pasha. After this little episode we took a pilot on board, who at once declared the passage of the strait impossible; so we scudded across the harbour into the open.

Here there was a heavy sea running, and our yacht rolled freely. Wasfi, who had hitherto been in a state of dumb misery, now leapt about, wept violently, and shrieked madly. His rolling eyes, distorted features, and savage yells were at first amusing; as were his cries: "Oh my broken heart, my crumbled liver! God blacken your faces, you dogs of sailors. O day dark as mud!" But finding no notice taken he cried out again, "Go back, go back, I conjure you in the name of God and his Prophet; ya Muslimîn, ya Muslimîn." At the same time he made the most frantic and desperate efforts to throw himself overboard. It took three or four of us to hold him. What with his struggles and his adjuration—the most solemn appeal in the language to the men of his creed—he gained his purpose, and we put back into smooth water. As we were walking up to the palace afterwards, he inveighed most bitterly against his fortune, which he said had ruined all the pleasure of Alexandria; for six weeks to come that sail had poisoned his life! "This day of mud has blackened forty days of milk! It was a fearful and extraordinary event; and, were it graven on the understanding, it were a lesson to him that needs admonishment. Verily to God we belong and unto Him we return; there is no escape from that which is decreed and predestined."

I may note in passing, that it is habitual with the Arabs thus to enamel their conversation with pious phrases; a practice far removed from intentional blasphemy or careless levity, and equally removed from intentional piety.

The Khedive at this time became rich in advice of one sort or another. One of the European consuls at Alexandria told Tewfik that Ismail used always to bribe people to cheer him as he drove through the streets, and once spent a large sum for this purpose; and the consul recommended the Khedive to follow his father's good example. Tewfik replied coldly, "You are strangely mistaken if you imagine that I should care for such hired demonstrations; if shows of loyalty do not come from the heart, they are worthless to me. I shall not condescend to obtain by bribery a result I should despise." That consul, I think, withdrew with air crestfallen. Next some Jew bankers came to congratulate the Khedive on the winding-up of the Commission of Liquidation. They dilated on the advantage to Egypt of the settlement, and at last said, "By and by, when the settlement has taken due effect, we shall be most happy to advance Your Highness money to any amount at seven per cent." The Khedive looked at them and replied, "I am very much obliged to you; it was your kindness which ruined my father, and nearly ruined Egypt. I have no need of your money, and do not intend availing myself of your services." They also retired, doubtless murmuring, like the discomfited Jew in the Arabian Nights, "Oh, Ezra! Oh Moses and the Ten Commandments! Oh Ezra's ass!" Thus, at any rate, Egypt was delivered from the children of Israel.

A great fête was given in honour of Sir Rivers Wilson and the Commission in the gardens of Râs-el-Tin palace, which were illuminated. There was a grand military procession by torchlight, and a procession of native trade-guilds. The latter was rather disappointing; the gardeners carried nosegays of flowers, but none of the other crafts had any emblem, though all had music. After this there was a grand illumination of the harbour and ships. The sight under the moonlight was splendid. Scores of little boats were moving about decked with lanterns; but the most picturesque of all were two Greek ships, with lofty prow and stern after the classical model, such as might have been used by the Greeks two thousand years ago here in this very harbour of Alexandria. I was rowed about for some time in a luxurious twelve-oared galley; and the remembrance of that Egyptian night upon the sea still lives in my mind with the remembrance of sunny days in a caïque upon the Bosporus, and of moonlight nights in a gondola at Venice.

Another evening I was invited to witness an Arab play at the Zizinia Theatre by the Khedive's order, he himself being present. It was a sad business. Four acts, each of an hour's duration, no changes of scenery, no plot, no action. First entered an old greybeard, who sat on a chair between two flowerpots, moaning and mumbling by the space of an hour. Enter next two wealthy sheikhs in native dress, smoking long jessamine pipes. They sat on chairs, one right and one left of the greybeard, and talked for an hour. When they retired, two fellahín came in; and, leaning each on his staff in identical attitudes, they also talked for an hour. They were followed by two of the "young Egypt" party, who likewise conversed for an hour. Their discourse was wholly political, and seemed desperately dull; but I confess I fled after the first act of this very Semitic drama.

Very many days about this time were spent at the hospitable houses of English friends at Ramleh. Even on the hottest afternoons one played lawn tennis on the sand-courts of the country. In Cairo, as before stated, one played tennis in the open during extreme heat: here the heat registered less by the thermometer, but was damper and more trying though less in intensity. Indeed, one hardly regarded the sun in playing, finding sunshine often preferable to the shade,—especially as the mosquitoes held the converse opinion. In the evening we dined in English fashion—a great relief after palace meals—but English fashion improved by the enfranchisement of tobacco.

Of the mosquitoes there were several tribes: the worst, perhaps, was a tiny species called by the Arabs "yâkul-uskut," or "bite and say nothing," so termed from the fact that they sound no clarion for their onset. Besides mosquitoes there abounded ants, scorpions, and tarantulas; snakes were fairly plentiful; and the harmless jerboa might sometimes be seen on the sky-line of a hill at sundown.

There was no more genial host in those days than poor Morice Bey, the debonair, merry, and chivalrous soldier who perished with Baker's Egyptian army near Trinkitat, less than three years after. In 1880 he was head of the Coastguard service, and one night after dinner talked a great deal about the smuggling that still flourishes. He said that it cost the Egyptian Government quite 100,000*l*. a year. The contraband trade was chiefly in tobacco from Syria, and was managed by the Greeks, who were aided even by their consuls. Lately the Greek consul at Port Said led a mob of five hundred compatriots to attack a party of coastguards who had seized some tobacco; and the consul during the scuffle fastened his teeth into the arm of an antagonist. Morice Bey saw the mark, and found that it corresponded with the setting of the consul's teeth exactly, and that the wound had a gap answering to a lost tooth. The smugglers even confessed that the tobacco was contraband; yet the upshot was that the coastguards got punished, and the smugglers let off, if not rewarded. At Alexandria Morice was out every night; and after many a sharp skirmish, in which he had often been under fire and had killed several smugglers, he had made that part of the coast too hot for them. But they had only to go thirty or forty miles eastward towards Rosetta, where they could land as much tobacco as they pleased, and get it conveyed by Beduins to inland towns. Morice had been six hundred miles *west* of Alexandria, and said that the coast all along is utterly desert, with only one place where there are trees. After six hundred miles the few Beduins to be found say that Egypt ends and Tripoli begins: they even point out a frontier. Along this desolate shore, however, may be met many pilgrims going and returning from Mecca to Morocco and Algiers. Their journey is a year's walking, during which time the miserable creatures depend for food on chance encounters with wandering tribes, and on scanty brackish wells for water. Vast numbers of course perish by the wayside. *Tantum religio potuit suadere malorum.* Yet the faith, the sense of duty, the self-devotion of such men deserve rather admiration than pity.

One of the greatest smugglers in Alexandria was Hussein Bey, commandant of Fort Pharos, a renegade Greek, brother of a tobacco-merchant in the city. He used to allow cargoes to be landed under the walls of his fortress; and once, when Morice Bey seized a quantity of tobacco at two o'clock in the morning, Hussein remarked coldly, "Yes, I seized it yesterday for you, and was going to hand it over to-day!" Formerly the Government allowed prize-money on captures of contraband; and in those days Morice Bey used to spend much of his life in the desert chasing and fighting Beduin caravans. In one such skirmish his little party of five had three horses killed and two men wounded; but he seized two thousand bales of tobacco. The Beduins generally ran away after a few shots had been exchanged. Now, however, the Government offers no reward for contraband taken in the desert, and the trade thrives. Morice Bey showed me a map of the Egyptian coastline, from which it was clear that only a small fraction is in any way guarded. "With my very small force," he said, "the work is hopeless." One of the great contraband dealers, whom I could name, tried to simplify matters by giving a bribe of 10,000*l.* to Morice Bey, who, needless to say, rejected the offer. The Greek shrugged his shoulders, and remarked, "My dear fellow, you are too English. What is the good of worrying yourself day and night, and risking your life in this manner? You never can touch us. I assure you that I can afford to spend 50,000*l.* at Cairo in counteracting your advice to the Government; and I tell you frankly, every letter and despatch you send to the ministry is copied, and received by me in duplicate; so that I always know what I have to do." This man owns a whole village on the Nile, where the people are exclusively engaged in receiving the smuggled tobacco as it comes across the desert, and in forwarding it along the river to the Greek traders scattered by the score in every part of Egypt.

The walk from Alexandria to Ramleh along the shore is very interesting to an antiquary. The sandy cliffs in places are steep, and show in section strata laid by the hand of time during generations of the Greek and Roman period. Volumes of ancient history are written there on the coast, but no one in Egypt ever dreams of reading a line. The walk took me about three hours leisurely strolling on a hot August afternoon. Greek and Roman remains lay all along the shore and under the sea. In the cliffs, which rise to about thirty feet in height, were continuous layers of broken brick and pottery, with here and there traces of solid masonry—rooms, baths, heating apparatus, earthenware boilers, &c. By the Round Tower, near the station, are ponderous masses of brickwork shaken in ruins, yet still showing remains of arches and other architectural details. The Silsilah Fort, standing at the end of a long mole, forms the eastern wing of the Old Harbour, while the western is formed by Fort Pharos, said to have been built by the great Harûn-er-Rashîd. At the landward gate of the causeway I demanded leave to enter. The two guards eyed me a moment in silence; then one took me apart, and whispered, "Is there bakshîsh?"

"There is," I replied.

"Good. Hand me the bakshîsh."

"No, my good friend," I said, "not till I have seen the fort."

"No one ever sees the fort; it is forbidden."

"True; but generosity opens the door of prohibition."

"But where is the generosity?"

"Be patient," I answered: "I am an Englishman, and my word is straight." The guard turned to his companion, repeating my words, "He says he is an Englishman, and his word is straight," and they at once let me pass. The causeway was originally defended by two lines of wall, six feet and four feet thick respectively, but is now much broken; and, as a high sea was running, I was unable to reach the fortress. But returning I gave the bakshish, which was folded in the hand, kissed, and raised to the forehead with all due ceremonial.

About a mile further I found remains of catacombs hewn in the rock and still bearing traces of plaster. I saw also in the middle of the cliff a black basalt flooring a foot thick; a fragment of a fine column; many pieces of marble, alabaster, and red porphyry. The most durable material seemed brickwork, united by a cement of pounded brick and shell mixed with lime. The strata in the sand were singularly level, showing no sign of disturbance by earthquake. At the Ramleh Palace a wall runs into the sea, so I had to leave the shore, passing over the famous battlefield to the little mosque where tradition says that Abercrombie's body was carried to rest. But I have often wondered why so little has been done to explore the rich remains of Alexandria.

Another day I visited the Lighthouse Fort at the west end of the Râs-el-tin promontory. No travellers or strangers are ever allowed there. The lighthouse is about thirty feet in diameter, and mounted by two hundred and forty steps. It is well built; for at the time of the bombardment a shell from the Inflexible struck the tower and made a great gap in its side, but the structure held together. From the top one gets a range of view quite out of proportion to the height. Below lies the harbour dotted with great ships, and the breakwater standing between a sea of stormy waves and a flashing mirror of calm water; beyond runs a long narrow ribbon of sand dividing the bay from Lake Mareotis; all the town with its palaces and minarets; an endless palm-grown shore east and west; inland the desert and northward the sea. All this in the golden glow of an Egyptian evening formed a scene strangely bright, strangely moving in its associations, and pathetic in its very splendour.

Near the deserted palace of Said Pasha on the opposite side of the harbour lie numerous catacombs well worth a visit. In this region are the so-called Baths of Cleopatra, with many genuine remains of baths, ovens, dwelling-chambers, and places of burial. The most remarkable relic, perhaps, is a rock-cut cavern, which looks much like an early Christian church and burial-place. It has a Doric portal with square engaged pilasters at the sides; the portal opens into a circular hall with a domed roof; and inside three other doorways lead into dark chambers, one in front and one at each side. In the frontward chamber one discovers yet another doorway opening into a smaller shrine which lies beyond, and which contains what may be the remains of an ancient altar. The plan is somewhat analogous to that of other early Coptic churches hewn in the rock.*

But more delightful than these solitary rambles were the Ramleh picnics. One day I specially recall, a day of scorching heat early in September. Even at nine o'clock in the morning and with a keffeiah over my head I got a little touch of sun, but soon recovered. We started towards Mandârah

* See "Ancient Coptic Churches of Egypt," Clarendon Press, Oxford, 1884, vol. ii. pp. 349 and 350.

about eleven o'clock, and went eastward, following the shore of Lake Abukîr, which lay on our right half-a-mile distant. The dark reach of level sand was varied here and there with curious formations, strewn sometimes with small pebbles, sometimes with tiny fragments of pottery, sometimes with dust of broken cockleshells. The lake shone like a mirror of pale dazzling blue; while here and there in the distance islands and capes were rendered visible by the palm-trees upon them, and Arab barges with their large three-cornered sails stood as if fixed in a dream. Far away, the waters faded imperceptibly into the sky, which on the horizon was, like the lake, of a pale whitish blue, while higher up and overhead the heaven glowed with the deep lustrous sapphire hue of an Egyptian summer. On our left at a short distance rose a continuous ridge of low sand-hills, dotted and crowned with palm-trees of all sizes. The sand here was like pure gold in colour; and the sun, now at the zenith, cast the shadows in such a manner that every leaf was repeated in a perfect ring round the foot of the palm-tree. Nothing could be more lovely than this golden knoll of sand with its rings of feathery shadow and its tufted palms laden with purple clusters of dates, the whole scene divided sharply at the sky-line from the field of cloudless blue above. To realize the colour of such skies one should always get a point of contrast well above the horizon.

As we left the ridge of hills, we passed through many changes of desert scenery, and presently found the sand thickly set with low bushes. These bushes were the haunt of Arab bird-catchers, who place limed twigs upon them, and lie hidden in rude shelters of palm-branches, watching to seize the birds as soon as they alight. Beccaficoes are what they prize the most; but they capture also quail, hoopoes, king of the quail, yellow thrush, hawks, and even sparrows.

When at length we reached Mandârah, a small Arab village, little boys came running out and saying "Will you take water?" After a two hours' ride under such a sun in the desert, we knew how delicious a draught from a cool, clear well could be; and we not only drank, but had pitchers of water poured over our heads. Then we separated in search of a place for lunch; lost each other for an hour in quest of the lunch-cart, which appeared to be hopelessly astray in the wilderness; but at last recovered the cart, and met together in a sheltered spot. Soon turkey and pigeon-pie, tongue, salad, and champagne—all the accessories of an English picnic—were spread on the ground; and we eat, watched by the natives with relentless curiosity. After lunch we strolled or sat by the shore for nearly three hours; then rode back with the sea on our right, the desert on our left, and palm-trees all about us.

Not less delightful were the moonlight rides and picnics along the coast. One night, after crossing spaces of undulating desert and threading our way through groves of palm, we would rest at a spot where great white waves were rolling up the beach; another time we had a midnight picnic at the Spouting Rocks, where fountains of spray seem to break from the ground; but always the night was enchanted, and the moonlight on sea and sand and palm was beautiful beyond description.

CHAPTER VI.

Conversations with the Khedive—Slave trade—Egyptian morals—
The Dôsah—The month of fasting—Ceremony at the palace—
Superstitious customs—Ramleh sportsmen—Story of the Sultan
—"Our own correspondent"—Story of Fakri Pasha—An
unpleasant journey.

FREQUENT conversations with the Khedive now gave me a closer insight not only into his character, which I learnt to respect and admire, but into the countless intrigues which beset him. I learnt also many curious phases of native custom little known to Europeans; for a keen eye, a prodigious memory, and a very taking manner of speech, render the Khedive the most pleasant and most instructive of talkers. Turâbi was often, though not always, present at these interviews; so that when English or French failed, Turkish was available to interpret.

Much of course was said about the slave-trade; and, if there is one conviction planted root and fibre in my mind, it is that the Khedive in his heart of hearts detests the system. I once showed him a letter in *The Times* from the secretary to the British and Foreign Anti-Slavery Society, in which a correspondent at Jeddah was cited to show the increase in the traffic since the departure of Colonel Gordon from the Sudân. The Khedive thought the fact likely, and deplored it. He told me that Mr. Malet had urged him to issue a sudden order briefly decreeing "All slaves are free"; but that he found it impossible to make such a revolution in a moment. The difficulty is that slavery is so interwoven not only with the harim system, but with the very religion of the Muslims, that it could not be withdrawn without unravelling the whole social fabric. The Khedive himself has never bought a single slave, though he had to take over some of his father's when he came to the throne. All his so-called slaves receive 2*l.* a month as wages, besides food and clothing. The abominations practised for the eunuch-trade are not exaggerated:* but the few survivors

* *Captis inter bella intestina pueris in Nubia uno ictu praeciduntur partes : tunc ipsi in terram medio tenus defossi relinquuntur ut sanguis sistatur vel, quod plerumque evenit, pueri miserrime moriantur. Ex illo vulnere adeo pauci convalescunt ut ex centum pueris vix quinque vivi supersint.*

are petted and caressed by the women, and often acquire great wealth and power. Thus Khalil 'Agha, chief eunuch to Ismail, died worth more than 100,000*l.* I asked the Khedive what would happen to the wives supposing there were no slaves and no guards to the harim. He said at once that the women would rush into every sort of licence. I replied that just at first there might be some abuse of a novel freedom; but after a while, when women were better educated, I saw no reason why they should not behave as well as European women.

The Khedive agreed that the one thing essential was education, and he has himself started a sort of high-school for girls in Cairo. But his idea of the Muslim women's morality is very low; he represents them as incessantly talking, dreaming, and scheming sensuality. In Turkey, he said, the ladies have much more freedom; they are scarcely veiled at all, and many go about the streets and even talk with men in the bazaars; but they are very virtuous. A Turk of high rank told me that once he was in the bazaars at Stambûl with a friend, when the latter, carried away by admiration for a lady of great beauty, tried to kiss her. She turned on him with fury, boxed both his ears, called him all the bad names in the language, and made such an uproar that he fairly took to his heels. It would be a natural retort to such a story that the man would not have made so bold had he thought to encounter so much virtue. But a Turk does not think in such cases. I have known a Turk to fling himself on the ground before a beautiful woman in the Park in London and beg her to trample upon her slave.

But, if the Egyptian women at present are in a very degraded condition, the men are no better. One day, when the English aquatic sports and swimming races were held in the harbour at Alexandria, the Khedive and Court were present out of compliment; but the pashas were quite astonished to find that there were no English ladies looking on, and remarked how their own womenfolk would like such an opportunity. One pasha however put his own oriental point of view with brutish plainness.*

I had means of knowing a good deal that went on in the harîms, and vouch for the fact that the influence of the women on the children is most deplorable. They have no reverence for tender years, and even before little boys and girls they talk and joke

---

* *Cur nos, inquit, ad ejusmodi spectaculum trahimur? Adeone incesti ridemur? Feminas potius exhibendas judicamus.*

about such things as no lady in England would even know. The same is true of the men. One bey used to think it amusing to instruct the poor little princes in immorality. Another used to do his best to make them idle by telling them in Turkish before my face, "If you don't like to do your lesson, remember you are princes, and can please yourselves." He knew that I could not understand his language, but the words were reported to me. Fortunately the princes had truer ideas of their duty. One day the younger, Mohammed 'Ali, was rather sulky and refused to work. "Come, prince," I said to him, "it must be done." 'Abbas Bey, the elder, at once caught me up, and said "Prince! he is no prince; he is a fellah." "Why do you say that?" I asked. "Why, because he is idle, and won't obey." The Khedive laughed loud and long on hearing this anecdote.

But to resume. The Khedive himself has the greatest horror of the harim, not merely because of the moral corruption, but also on account of the ignorant, fanatical, and superstitious ideas of the women. He told me strange things scarcely to be written even in a "learned language."* One well-

* *Domus* esse in urbe *quas potentiores feminae, Messalinae* more, *frequentent. Alexandriae autem* apud *humillimam plebem mores* vel

known lady of rank in Cairo had emancipated herself from native seclusion, and went about like a European. She was a most imperious person, and bullied her husband shamelessly by reason of her wealth and title. If he dared to remonstrate, she would order twenty slaves to beat him.

I learnt that the Khedive belongs, like most Turks, to the sect called Hanafi. He told me that it is a principle of this sect to admit of education and progress, and that he personally considered the social and religious ideas of the people capable of development. A generation ago a Turkish lady would have been anathematised for speaking a word of French or English; whereas now many ladies speak foreign languages. Yet Mohammed 'Ali the Great was a most zealous reformer. One story which the Khedive told of him is worth recording. Being very anxious to further education, Mohammed 'Ali tried hard to persuade the natives to send their children to school, enlarged on the advantages mental and worldly of instruction, and promised handsome rewards. All in vain; the pashas could not see the use of worrying

pravissimos obtinere : quoties enim vir amicum hospitio exceperit, nec filiae suae nec conjugis castitati parcere. This, however, is by no means true of the fellahin in the country districts, who are simpler and better folk.

themselves and spending their money on their children. Thereupon the Viceroy, persuasion having failed, changed his tactics, ordered all children in Cairo to be dragged with irons round their necks to school daily, and there literally chained to their lessons—compulsory education with a vengeance.

This talk about reforms gave me a long-desired opportunity. With very little preface, I asked, " Will not Your Highness be able to stop the Dôsah next year ? "—that horrible ceremony of riding over the dervishes, of which an account has been given earlier in this book.* He replied, no, not next year, he feared ; it was cruel and barbarous, but he had no power to abolish an ancient religious custom which had taken hold of the people's imagination. I ventured to differ, remarking that he was ruler of Egypt and had only to say firmly, " I will not allow this to continue," and it would cease. The people, I added, knew by proof how he studied their welfare, and would not be alienated ; moreover the ceremony was not a part of the Muslim religion, but only a local heresy. The Khedive answered that the educated few would rejoice in the suppression of the practice, but the ignorant masses would have their

---

* See pp. 38—44 supra.

fanaticism stirred dangerously. One must have patience. In a few years, perhaps two or three, something might be done. "I am *ashamed* of the Dôsah," he said, with emphasis, "and would gladly suppress it." Then I cited the case of the Juggernaut festival in India, and remarked that the fear of kindling excessive animosities had proved groundless.

"That," said the Khedive, "was a dreadful thing, involving loss of life; here no one is seriously wounded. A certain number suffer bruises and contusions, nothing more." Thereupon I told him how I had seen the poor wretches mangled and writhing. He said, "The horse is not shod with iron; I gave special orders that it should not be."

"Pardon me," I replied, "but after the ceremony I went myself and examined the horse's feet, and with my own eyes I saw that the horse had iron shoes."

The Khedive thought I must be mistaken, but I was quite positive on the point. He added that he made inquiries from the doctors of the dervishes, and could only learn that there were a number of bruises. These doctors, of course, conceal the truth: but I again described the sights which I had witnessed, and which the Khedive from his tent had been unable to see. The Khedive had also inquired of the sheikh of the dervishes whether he would not like as well to be drawn by six horses through Cairo between lines of soldiers; but the sheikh replied that the people would not be satisfied. So for the while the subject dropped. It was two o'clock in the morning; for, during the month of Ramadhan, the Khedive generally sent for me at midnight and kept me talking for two or three hours. He now asked me, laughing, whether I would keep the fast. "No, Highness," I replied, "and if I turn Muslim, it must be when the fast is over."

It was on Friday 6th August that Ramadhan began that year, and I received the cheerful news that while it lasted no breakfast or luncheon would be provided in the palace. For during the fast a Muslim may not even smell food or tobacco between sunrise and sunset. The month dated from sunset, and was received with a salvo of twenty-one guns from the frigate in harbour. At nine o'clock a *levée* was holden of native notables, 'ulema, and Beduin sheikhs, altogether a picturesque company. During Ramadhan a large tent was pitched in the palace gardens, and occupied by three or four 'ulema whose duty it was to chaunt verses from the Korân through the night without ceasing. Every evening, too, just after dinner, there was held a ceremony somewhat resembling family prayers. Two 'ulema first shouted from the palace-steps the formal sing-song call to prayer; then all the courtiers, officers, and domestics assembled in the hall and went through a ritual of set words and postures for half-an-hour. My friend Turâbi Bey refused to fast or to pray, and so did Sâlim Pasha. They were worried a good deal by the others, but said flatly that they did not believe in fasting, and as for the praying, Sâlim Pasha remarked to me, "After a good dinner I cannot go through those gymnastics." Turâbi told them to mind their own business, that he was responsible to God for his actions, not to them. They were ready to tear him to pieces, but in their hearts hated the fasting and the praying as much as Turâbi.

Their worship is a mere fetish; they are righteous as long as they go through their forms and their lip-service and give a few piastres in alms to beggars. An equally devout but cheaper practice is to feed and clothe the naked and hungry with fine phrases, such as, "God is merciful," "May God give you," "May God open a better way." They have no idea of sin, nor of religion as a spiritual power.

One night, *par plaisanterie*, the Khedive remonstrated with Turâbi for not fasting, and said he ought to keep Ramadhan for one day at least; "Indeed," he continued, "I command you, Turâbi; only I must have you locked up or I am afraid you would eat and smoke in your own room in spite of your promise." Poor Turâbi, taking it all *au sérieux*, pleaded most pitifully, alleging delicate health, weak nerves, and shattered constitution; then, failing these excuses, he had recourse to flattery, saying that everybody noticed how bright and pleasant the Khedive's face always looked in spite of the fast, while so many other countenances were rendered sour and gloomy or even savage. The whole scene produced much laughter.

But I was very glad when from the shore at Ramleh I watched the setting of the sun which closed the wretched month of Ramadhan. Everybody had suffered by it. The natives lose every atom of energy and temper. They turn day into night, breaking fast at sunset, taking lunch at midnight, and supping an hour before sunrise. During the day they are sleepy, comatose, and intensely surly. We Europeans had to make shift as we could by going a mile to the town for our food. I often saw Beduins watching the sun's globe till the last of the rim plunged in the sea, when they lit their cigarettes and devoured grapes or dates or such scanty food as they possessed. In the palace all rushed at gun-fire to a heavy meal, but they assembled in the ante-rooms at least half-an-hour before the time, and spent the interval in drawing out and replacing their watches. They count and dispute and prove by elaborate argument every minute; time dies hard thus nursed by forty watches. The yawns, too, were prodigious. When a man yawned he would cover his mouth, not to conceal the action but to prevent an evil spirit from jumping down his throat, and he would mutter the talisman, " I seek God's protection from Satan the accursed."

Next morning dawned the festival of the lesser Bairam. Waking at five o'clock I saw beneath my windows long lines of white-clad soldiers showing dimly in the last shadows of night. As the sun rose, I noticed just before the palace-steps a large square place laid with matting, on which were strewn gorgeous carpets. At one corner was raised a wooden pulpit, draped in red cloth and decked with two large purple flags. Many servants and others were already praying, but the four thousand troops stood motionless. Now the ministers, with Riaz Pasha at their head, the dignitaries and sheikhs assembled, pulled off their boots and ranged themselves in rows upon the carpets, all facing eastward. The boots were left near the edge of the matting; there were the top-boots of the body-guard, the patent boots of the ministers, the yellow or red shoes of the merchants, and a very odd figure they cut, all standing empty in order and waiting for their owners.

The company now fell upon their knees, the front rank being composed exclusively of 'ulema, or religious elders, who sang together a low chaunt. Suddenly the four bands of music clashed out the khedivial hymn and the troops presented arms. The sun, now risen above the palace walls, struck the tops of the acacias as the Khedive was seen descending the marble steps with his retinue. At the foot of the staircase two slaves removed his shoes. Walking on to the carpet he knelt at the head of the line of 'ulema, the chief of whom now began chaunting the Muslim form of prayer, the whole congregation saying the words after him and repeating his postures. When it was ended, he cried, " Peace be with you!" and mounted the pulpit. All remained kneeling during the sermon, which lasted only five minutes. As the service closed, the bands struck up again and the artillery of the forts thundered. The troops passed in review and the usual *levée* began. All Muslims on this morning embrace each other at their first meeting. My servant came into my room beaming with pride in his new silk robes, and made the proper obeisance, *i. e.*, lightly touched my fingertips, then kissed his hand and raised it to his forehead, and touched breast, lips, and forehead again. A native form of homage to the Khedive is kissing the hem of his garment or kissing his boots. Even the great pashas of the Court do this on occasion. Kissing the hem of the garment is a common mark of homage among women also in the harims.

The little princes in speaking to each other have no pet names, but use the full name and title. Thus, 'Abbas Bey calls out "Mohammed 'Ali Bey!" and the answer is "Effendum," *i. e.*, "Your Highness."

Perhaps here I may put together some native customs and ideas which I learned while at Alexandria. Even in the highest families strange superstitions linger. For some time before the birth of a certain noble youth his mother used to go every night with her handmaidens to a room in which a censer of burning incense stood upon the floor. The girls placed themselves in a ring round it, and the mother solemnly stepped seven times across the smoking censer. So when the baby was born they carried him seven times round the censer. In the same house a kind of divination was practised as follows. A fire was kindled, and on it was prepared a cauldron of molten lead; a girl standing in front of the fire—her body well padded and her face covered with an iron mask—ladled out the lead, and threw it into a vessel of water. So from the shapes which the metal took they presaged good or evil fortune for the boy. They also burned a sort of pod which cracked and popped loudly, and the sound was thought to destroy the power of the evil eye.

The evil eye is the worst bugbear of these people. A woman coming from market covers up her basket very carefully on the way home, lest the evil eye strike her goods. Fish is specially subject to the malign power, and if struck loses all its flavour. Among the fellahin our St. George and Dragon sovereign is much prized and treasured, because they regard the figure as a talisman against the evil eye; native doctors, too, use it in a charm to cure ophthalmia. St. George is of course an Egyptian saint, much venerated still by the Copts, and the Arab superstition must be a relic of a very early Christian idea. Many believe that a man with the evil eye can, by a glance, kill a camel. Charms or amulets against it are very numerous: sometimes a little silver hand placed between a horse's eyes; sometimes a tiny parchment bag with texts from the Korán fastened round the neck of man or beast; or beads or pieces of tinsel fastened on a child's head-dress. So, if a man has a headache, he will hang a piece of bread from his tarbûsh over the temple; if his eyes are bloodshot or sore, he suspends a piece of raw meat between them to draw out the evil.

The imposture of snake-charming is well-known, but very cleverly managed. Wasfi told me a story of an attempt he made to find out the trick. A party of friends hired a professional charmer to visit a house, whence he undertook to clear out the serpents by incantation. Ere he entered the rooms, they stripped him, and examined every inch of his clothing without result, and they never lost sight of him for a moment. In a well-lighted room he could do nothing; but in a dim chamber he worked his spells with such success that he drew forth no less than seven long serpents, which came out hissing one by one from beneath the furniture. One of the company suddenly said "I wish to examine that snake," and, in spite of the wizard's frantic warning that to touch it was death, he caught it. He saw at once that it was a mountain-snake, not a house-snake, and that it was fangless. The mystery remained how the charmer had contrived to bring his pets into the house. Thus baffled in their curiosity, the young fellows rushed upon the man, threw him on the floor, and threatened to bastinado him unless he revealed his secret. He whined and howled most pitiably, said it was his profession, and that he had no other way of earning his bread; till at last, moved by his tears, they released him and let him depart with his secret.

The Arabs believe that the sources of the Nile are in Paradise; while the Turks in Egypt and Muslims generally firmly hold the doctrine that the earth rests upon the horns of a bull. They say that, when God frowns upon the bull, it moves uneasily, and the earth quakes. To ask what the bull stands upon is a silly and impious question; for the Muslim creed does not assign him even a tortoise for his footstool. Vergil's *caelifer Atlas* seems a higher conception. The world nevertheless is firmly fixed upon the bull's horns. "Why," said a grey-bearded pasha, "if the earth moved round the sun, all the pots and pans would be flying about! Only infidels talk such nonsense; God's curse upon them!"

An English lady told me that once the wife of a distinguished native showed her the picture of a strange beast—a four-winged horse, having the head and breast of a woman, richly adorned with jewelled necklets. "Look," she said, "this is the horse that will carry me to Paradise." "Oh! what a beautiful animal," was the reply; "and shall I go to heaven on a horse like that?" "No, indeed; you Christian will be lucky if you get there on a donkey."

Most of the pashas about the Court believed that the sky formed a solid roof to the world, and in it the stars were merely marks set to denote human destinies. When they saw a falling star, they exclaimed, "Another man is dead."

Speaking of things astronomical I may here record a very picturesque expression in use among the modern Greeks. When the sun has set, they say, εβασίλευσε, his reign is over; and of the dead also they use the same term—his kingdom is past.

One evening, while I was at dinner, a servant entered with frightened face saying that something awful had happened to the moon, that it was turned to blood and gave no light, though high in the heavens. I went out, and saw the moon three-parts overcast with a beautiful rose-crimson veil, shading off to pale green and yellow. "Our Lord only knows what has done this," said the black. All round the palace, and from the barracks nigh, long-drawn shouts were rising mingled with the beat of tomtoms and clanging of iron bars; while here and there 'ulema were chaunting prayers. Later that night I asked a donkey-boy what it all meant, and he answered that once every year the moon makes a "fantasia" of that kind to amuse itself. Subsequently, however, in a more serious mood he said, "God covers the moon with blood; the people pray, and it passes."

Muslim women cover their heads and faces when they pray; it is at all times wrong and sinful for them to let a single hair of their heads be seen by a man. The eyes of course they expose when walking; but they are very careful not to leave the mouth uncovered. Rich mothers often send sick children round to several mosques, in order that prayers may be said over them in holy places; and the child is often made to lay its hand on a tomb of special sanctity, while prayers are uttered. On the other hand some mothers are very cruel. Even in the best houses there is a form of punishment used for children and slaves which is very barbarous. The culprit's hands are bound tightly together, and then held above his head by a strong cord fastened to a hook in the wall. The Khedive told me that as a child he twice suffered this punishment for seven hours continuously.

A European lady related that once, when she was paying a visit to a native, she found her hostess in tears, and on asking the cause was informed, "I am miserable because my husband has not given me a fish."

"Not given you a fish? But what do you want a fish for?"

"Oh, don't you know that at the beginning of every year our husbands give us a fish in token that they will not divorce us during the year: and this time my husband has given me none." This curious custom does not seem to be mentioned by Lane or to be known to residents in Egypt.

While at Alexandria I witnessed the reception of a new consul-general, M. Rhangabé, representing Greece. The usual order of ceremony was followed.

Two state carriages sent by the Khedive brought the consul from his hotel to the palace, where he was received with a military salute and music. Being ushered into the presence he read an address to the Khedive, who gave a written reply and invited his guest to be seated. Coffee was then served and the pipe of state was brought, the long-stemmed shibûk, not the nargileh. In ordinary life nothing but cigarettes or cigars is seen in the palace, but even on state occasions the Khedive never departs from his rule as a non-smoker. After some conversation the Khedive presented the consul with a gold-hilted scimetar; and an Arab horse caparisoned in native fashion, with high-backed saddle, embroidered saddle-cloth, and gorgeous reins, awaited him outside. This gift of a sword and a steed was strictly in accordance with ancient usage.

By the way, the orientals detest nothing more than movement, activity in a man or action in a horse. In a beast for riding their idea of perfection is a steady swing of the foreleg, so straight and even that the rider may drink a cup of coffee in mid-trot without spilling a drop. This result they accomplish by training colts to trot with heavy leaden weights round their forefeet. A horse so broken (called in Turkish *rahwân*) carries a fat, comfortable saddle, on which a fat, comfortable pasha may ride without being shaken about, and such a beast fetches a high price. It is the next best thing to a horse with wooden legs on wheels; in fact, an armchair on the back of a four-wheeled horse is the Turkish equestrian ideal.

A European practice—not English, happily—shall make the last bead on this motley rosary of customs. Towards the end of September quails arrive daily in great numbers from over the sea. Their flight is always timed to land them soon after sunrise, and they come whirring in like driven partridges. Yet they are so wearied out with their long journey that they often cannot stop or steer, and dash against walls and houses. When they alight safely, they hide among the wild ice-plants or garden-shrubs near the sea, and there rest a full day to recover their strength. But the Beduins spread long nets at points of vantage on the shore, with a mesh so fine that the quails get caught by the neck. Thence they are rescued alive and supplied by the dozen for Ramleh "sportsmen." A Ramleh shooting-party is a curious sight. It takes place generally on Sunday in a garden or walled inclosure. The party all sit on chairs, including the ladies, who are present to encourage their knights in the manly pastime. A Beduin throws the quails one by one into the air, and each sportsman has his shot in turn, and of course avoids the needless exertion of rising from his chair. The excitement is rendered more exciting by betting, and a ring of roughs surrounds the ground to slaughter the escaped birds. Such is the delight of the Alexandrian *chasseur*, Greek, French, and Italian.

At the end of July the Khedive had gone for a day to Cairo to be present at the cutting of the bank which floods the Nile canal; but otherwise there was no breaking away from Alexandria. He told me that the ceremony of throwing a mud figure into the water was duly observed. Tradition tells that in ancient times a virgin was thus sacrificed, but that the Caliph Omar abolished the barbarous rite. Arab historians (added the Khedive) record nothing but good of Omar; they say for instance that the great library of Alexandria was burnt, not by his orders, but by the Greeks, to prevent it falling into Omar's hands!

But, though the life flowed smoothly enough, it became more and more interesting as I got to know His Highness better. One evening I showed him an extraordinary statement made by Mr. Gladstone in Parliament (July 23rd, 1880), that "for misgovernment and unscrupulous maladministration it was difficult to find anything worse than the case of Egypt; yet Egypt was not considered hopeless, because there was not the evil of religious ascendancy." The Khedive was not less amazed than annoyed; I agreed with him in thinking the statement most unfair after all that had been done lately for good government. The latter clause, too, seemed unintelligible. No religious ascendancy in Egypt! The Khedive closed the subject by saying, "Mr. Malet must see this; it tallies ill with his despatches." He went on to tell me that he had many letters from Constantinople showing that native feeling was very bitter against Mr. Gladstone, while the Russians were delighted with the course of English policy. Just at that moment there was a Russian corvette in harbour, the officers of which had been to visit the Khedive in the morning. When the Khedive addressed them in French, they betrayed an open-mouthed amazement; one even said, " Why, Your Highness speaks French excellently!" They wondered, too, at the furniture and the beauty of the palace; and nearly bounded from their seats when the Khedive spoke in English. Altogether they appear to have lost their manners.

But to return to the Sultan. His Majesty about this time lived in one continual panic. He sat up till five o'clock every morning with his ministers; and had holden deep consultations with his astrologers concerning the surrender of Janina and the territory awarded to Greece by the Berlin Conference. The astrologers professed that they could not read the fates; which made the Sultan white with anger. "One thing, however, is clear," said the Khedive; "English influence is at its lowest." He confirmed the story that the Sultan had been subventioning a Turkish paper at the Government press to publish inflammatory articles against English rule for distribution among the Muslims of India; and that the whole of the Turkish Court party were in favour of Russia. We discussed the probable future of Turkish rule; and the sage conclusion we reached was—in the words of Turâbi Bey—that "the dominion of Turkey is numbered!" The Khedive expressed a hope that in such an event Egypt would be able to stand alone, becoming a sort of Belgium, and he dwelt much on the subject.

His sister, the Princess, had just been refused permission to land at Stambûl, as they feared she had come to intrigue instead of to recover her health. A letter just received from that city told the Khedive that a certain one of the 'ulema had mounted a minaret, and declaimed loudly against the injustice and oppression of the Government. The authorities heard of it, and promptly sent men to bring him down. "Stop," he said, "I have three words more;" and he cried aloud to the crowd below, "O Sultan of Islâm, listen to my words! If you do not mend your government and do justice, you and your empire shall perish." His arrest followed; then came the question, what to do with him? The Sultan wished to banish him. "No," replied Said Pasha; "if you do that, you will have the English ambassador meddling. Let us say that he is mad, and shut him up in a mad-house." There the poor fellow doubtless still lies, unless death has released him. The same letter announced that the astrologers now gave nothing but evil auguries against the Sultan, adding that he is no true Muslim, or he would kill all the Christians.

It is usual for the Khedive of Egypt shortly after his accession to the throne to make a visit of homage to the Sultan. But the Controllers in this instance forbade the journey, on account of the enormous bakshish which has to be given to the great pashas and their ruler at Stambûl. The cost would hardly have been less than 500,000*l.* in mere presents; for the Khedive and his family have not only to scatter a dew of diamonds and rubies at random on the thirsty Court, but there are certain large plants which require a whole river of gold for their refreshment. Upon the accession of Tewfik, the Porte wished to abolish the title of Khedive, and to make the ruler of Egypt a mere provincial governor. But the Powers objected to the proposal; and at last Tewfik received a letter offering the imperial firman for 20,000*l.* The terms were vigorously rejected, with the reply that the days of bakshish were over. But, as the firman still lingered, the Powers gave a hint that, if it were not forthcoming, Egypt could declare her independence. This settled the matter.

Ibrahim Pasha, brother of the Khedive, was anxious at this time to return to Egypt from England, and Lord Granville telegraphed to Mr. Malet asking if permission could be given. The Khedive referred the question to Riaz Pasha, who thought Ibrahim's presence dangerous to the country. This reply incensed Ibrahim—oddly enough against England; so he went off to Paris in dudgeon. Meanwhile the Egyptian princess, to whom he was betrothed and who possessed 40,000*l.* a year, became engaged to

Daûd Pasha. Prince Ibrahim was educated at Woolwich, where he rendered himself pleasant and popular.

The scheme for farming the Daira lands was in August again thrust upon the Khedive in a very impudent manner by its English promoters. One of them wrote in conjunction with a German banker saying that he now required a lease of only one half the lands; and he threatened, in the event of a refusal, that he would hurl all the engines of his power against the Egyptian Government. He was, he said, master of a great party in the state; the English consul, the English parliament, the English Cabinet were all slaves of his lamp; in fine, he threatened to overthrow the Khedive. I assured His Highness that he need not greatly regard this idle chatter; that English ministers were not very ready to push private enterprise, much less to take extreme and extremely unjust measures to carry it through. But at the same time another Englishman concerned in the venture declared to Turâbi Bey in violent language, that if the Egyptian Government did not yield he would oust them, ruin them, rend them in pieces. This Turâbi of course reported to the Khedive. What made things worse was that strong official pressure was again used to further the scheme, as I ere long discovered. It failed, however; and the promoters concealed their discomfiture under a report that the ministers rejected the plan for want of sufficient bribing; a report which was doubly false.

In truth, as the Khedive said, the days of bakshish were over at Court. He assured me that a correspondent of one of the great London papers—a paper which would curl with horror at the intelligence—offered to write articles favourable to His Highness and his *régime* for the modest stipend of 200*l*. a month. The Khedive flatly refused, saying that he was not afraid of the truth, nor of lies. Another time a German official of some standing in Egypt offered to import some fine horses for the Khedive, meaning, of course, to charge an unconsidered trifle for commission. The offer was declined with thanks; and in telling these stories the Khedive remarked, "Beggars are beginning to understand that things are changed, and that there is little chance for them now."

But, if the ministers were above corruption, on some subjects they possessed ideas curiously unenlightened, as may be gathered from the following anecdote. Fakri Pasha, Minister of Justice, was detected sending letters to the wife of Ahmed Bey Neshât, nephew of the murdered Mufettish. Ahmed was a fine-looking young fellow in the Khedive's service; his wife, who was reported marvellously beautiful, had been a slave of the ex-Khedive Ismail, who showed kindness to her even after her marriage. One day in the middle of August Fakri was driving in the Shubra Avenue with a friend, when Ahmed approached the carriage, and, after some angry words, struck Fakri several violent blows across the face with a cane—a most praiseworthy but most unusual proceeding in Egypt. Public opinion universally approved of Ahmed's courage; not so Fakri nor his colleagues in the Cabinet. On the 26th the whole body of ministers with the Prime Minister at their head came to see the Khedive. All the world had been saying that Fakri ought to be dismissed from office; the ministers would not only not hear of his dismissal, but they threatened that unless Ahmed were sent to exile and imprisonment in the Sudân, (which means death,) they would resign in a body! They said—Riaz Pasha said—that unless an example were made of Ahmed, any one might come up to a minister and strike him with impunity.

Such were their ideas of justice and of their own sanctity.

The predicament was serious, because there really was no other man capable of filling Fakri's place except Sherif Pasha, whom the Powers would not have tolerated. The Khedive's sense of right naturally revolted from the monstrous suggestion of sending Ahmed to the Sudân. I felt sure that the threat of resignation was a mere weapon of coercion; and, on the other hand, it was clear that the curtain ought not to fall on Fákri in the pose of injured innocence triumphant. It was therefore arranged that Ahmed should be dismissed from the Daira, but shortly afterwards compensated by another appointment; while an order was sent to Fakri, that, although he retained his office, he had incurred His Highness's severe displeasure, and was forbidden to come near the Court for three months without special command.

This incident naturally gave rise to a discussion on the harim system at a dinner at which I was present at Ramleh. Among the company was the English Controller, who stated that in India the Hindoos, as well as Muslims, guard their women very strictly but without eunuchs: yet in India the conditions of seclusion are fast relaxing. Some of the guests present argued that in Egypt it was wrong for English ladies to visit the harims, thus countenancing a vicious system, while others maintained that the example of English freedom could not fail to act as a solvent against native prejudice. For my own part, I found that I knew more of harim life and customs than any one present, as I had special sources of information; but for obvious reasons I contributed little of such knowledge to the discussion. My opinion was, that, if English ladies knew what they were doing, they would not sacrifice their self-respect by paying such visits. No doubt the example of their freedom would be envied, but no Muslim mind associates such freedom with virtue.

Returning from Ramleh that evening I reached Râs-el-Tîn palace at midnight, just in time to answer the Khedive's summons. I found him alone, but after a while Turâbi entered, bringing an article from *The Pall Mall Gazette* on "Recent Progress in Egypt." This the Khedive read aloud, then rendered into French, sentence by sentence, to be sure of hitting the meaning. At the words "This had given rise to the belief that he hates Europeans," he said energetically, "That is not true; it is not true; I do not hate Europeans!" But on the whole he was much pleased with the article, which rendered his honest efforts for good some justice.

The subject was followed out for some time, then, as opportunity offered, I opened another, the cruelty of natives to animals. The Khedive at once agreed that there was need for a very great change of feeling on the matter. I told him, what he well knew, the way in which donkeys are made to suffer by the savage bits, the tight breeching-straps, and the heavy sticks employed against them; he added that many boys have a short cane with an iron spike at the end when ladies are riding, because they have to lead them instead of driving them from behind. Once I saw an Arab with a pole balanced on his shoulder and at each end a dozen or more live ducks tied by the legs. Cats seem generally treated with kindness. Dogs, of course, even in the cities, are half wild, having no fixed home, but living in tribes, each of which has its own quarter of the town and fiercely resents the intrusion of any member of another clan. They serve as monuments and models of all that is despicable and detestable to the Arab mind—witness the well-known phrases, "Dog of a Christian," "Dog of a Jew," and the like. A favourite quotation of the natives gives a neat summary of such abuse. Their expression is,

"As saith the poet,

"'He is a dog, the son of a dog, and a dog was his grandsire; no good is in a dog, the offspring of a dog.'"

At the time of the bombardment of Alexandria an Arab might often be seen in Cairo leading a dog by a string fastened round its neck, and stopping at the corners of the streets to beat the poor brute savagely with a stick, crying aloud, "O you accursed dog Simûr! O dog of dogs, Simûr!"*

Yet as scavengers dogs receive a sort of kicking tolerance. For the same reason some few birds, such as storks and kites, are unmolested, while others in the country, such as the ibis and the hoopoe, are protected by a superstition which makes them the abode of departed souls. But on the whole the Arab has no sympathy with animals; the only real affection he betrays is for the flies and noxious parasites that infest his person. Yet he has such an odd way of saying and doing things that one's anger often collapses in a sense of humour. Once I saw a donkey-boy whose donkey was taking a wrong

---

* *i.e.* Admiral Seymour, who commanded the British Fleet.

turning. He rushed to the front, rained blows about the animal's eyes, and exclaimed, "Ah, you son of a dog, how long have I been teaching you the streets of Cairo?"

The Khedive hoped to educate native ideas, and spoke as one warmly interested. But it was now two o'clock in the morning, and gunfire sounding the hour of the Ramadhan supper bade me withdraw.

I omitted to mention one feature of this eastern life which gave it a touch of the Arabian Nights, if other touches were wanting. This was the Court story-teller, and it was in the long nights of Ramadhan that he plied his profession. Often when I obeyed the midnight summons to wait on Effendina, I found Osman the story-teller with him, reciting or reading stories. Generally he had a list of short titles on a paper and read them out, the Khedive asking for any tale he fancied. This amusement, however, never lasted long, and Osman soon retired.

One evening I specially remember towards the end of my stay in Alexandria—one of the most lasting scenes of a time rich in scenes to be remembered. I was sent for just after midnight and found the Khedive in the open air on the grand balcony outside the Dome Room. The dome under which this magnificent saloon lies is a landmark familiar to all who have ever entered Alexandria harbour. The floor of the room is inlaid with ivory, ebony, and sandal-wood, and the corridors are also floored with a parquet of costly woods. But it is the splendour of that summer night that dwells in the memory. The balcony overlooks the great harbour, which then was under the light of a full moon, and nothing could surpass in still beauty the wide stretch of moonlit waters, with the dim forms of great ships in the distance, while to the left the white houses and minarets shone like a city in dreamland. Comparing Cairo and Alexandria together, the Khedive, pointing with pride to the scene, said, "Where will you find anything like that in Cairo?" He is himself very fond of Alexandria, but all the pashas and people about him were fretting sorely after Cairo. During this interview, pacing up and down the balcony, the Khedive discoursed upon matters of interest and amusement, some of which are elsewhere recorded and others duly consigned to silence.

But at last even for the pashas it rang to evensong at Alexandria, and on the 16th September the Court returned to Cairo. My orders were to be at the station at 6 a.m. With difficulty I got a piece of stale bread and a glass of water for breakfast, and arrived at the station at the time appointed. There it was necessary to wait two hours; for H.H. the Princess, in whose suite I was to travel, started at eight o'clock. In the compartment with me were the Khedive's Master of Horse and the young princes' doctor,—both agreeable companions; but, just as the train was moving, in jumped to my speechless horror a couple of eunuchs who had missed their places.

Towards Ramleh I saw a friend in the desert, and leant out of the window waving a handkerchief. At once frantic alarm in the carriage; the Master of Horse called me wildly by name, the doctor tugged at my coat-sleeve, the eunuchs shrieked; but I took no notice. When a curve in the line hid my friend from view, I sat down again and said, " Well, what is the matter?" " Oh," they answered, "you should not behave like that: the Princess might have been looking out of the window and might have thought you were making signals to her." I could not help laughing, to me their view of the case was so utterly astonishing. After more than two hours of unbearable dust and heat, we stopped for five minutes, and dishes of food, together with a vessel of muddy water, were thrust into the carriage. No knives, forks, or plates, and only one glass for the whole company. Uneatable eatables fouled by black fingers, and the cup mouthed by thick-rolled lips, were offered to me, but I naturally preferred to continue starving and to let the dust choke my parched and burning throat. The others all plunged their paws emulously into dish after dish; they gobbled their meat and gulped their drink, giving thanks the while to Allah. Subsequently, I obtained a few grapes and a morsel of ice; then leaned back and smoked a cigar to cover my disgust.

At this time of year the Delta landscape is perhaps at its best; the rice and sugar-cane stand high and luxuriant, the maize is just in its first feathery bloom, thousands of acres are covered with the beautiful cotton-plant, now bright with yellow flowers; and all the channels are full of water, on which the lotus lies lazily resting in immemorial splendour.

CHAPTER VII.

Summer and Winter—Riaz Pasha—The Dôsah again—Slavery and England—The splendour of the Mufettish—Colonel Gordon—Bribing *The Times*—The Khedive and his father—Ismail and Russia.

CAIRO is always charming, and, much as one missed the sea-breezes, it was impossible not to share in some degree the pashas' delight at returning. Two days after our arrival, I learnt on good authority that summer was over, from a little dialogue which took place in the Ceremonies. The Master of the Horse, entering about four o'clock, saluted an aged courtier, and after due formalities of greeting said, " Honourable pasha! I hope your Excellency has slumbered well."

" Praise be to God, I need no slumber now."

" God is merciful, O Excellency, but how can you do without slumber?"

"Custom, my friend, is custom; and God cool your eyes with this knowledge. But it was written that I should never slumber during the daylight in winter."

As the thermometer registered 90° in the shade, despite a strong wind blowing, I thought the good pasha showed the temper of a salamander. In reality there are only three cool months: December, January, and February.

But the nights now were not unbearably hot, and many pleasant evenings we spent sitting in the gardens at Ismailia Palace. The first evening I went down and sat with Turâbi talking. Presently Prince Mahmûd entered, and drawing a chair near us poured forth his views on military matters for half-an-hour. Then came Riaz Pasha, Prime Minister, who after an interview with the Khedive joined us in the garden, sat a while, and retired saluting the prince with particular unction. A few minutes later the Khedive sent for Turâbi and me. We sat on the marble terrace before the hall. After contrasting the view with that from the balcony at Râs-el-Tin, the Khedive went on to speak of Riaz. The Prime Minister was highly delighted with his entertainment by a certain Mr. ——, who had bidden him to a banquet, and made a most flattering speech in his honour. Thereupon Riaz wished to promote his host to a richer appointment in the service. This, however, the Khedive refused to sanction. Another great source of pleasure to Riaz just then was a letter he had received from Sir Rivers Wilson, praising him and giving him credit for the suppression of the slave-trade. At this the Khedive was annoyed, and said, "Look at the facts; Riaz has a house full of unpaid slaves, and I have not one; but, because he has been in Europe and spoken smoothly to the English Government, he wins a wrong reputation. I hope to visit Europe myself, when perhaps more justice will be done to my policy. Sir Rivers Wilson also writes to me reminding me of my great power and my independence of my ministers. But it is essential for the interests of the country that we work together; if the people think that I have no confidence in my ministers, or my ministers in me, government will be impossible."

At this point Mustapha brought a telegram from Riâf Pasha, Colonel Gordon's successor at Khartûm, saying that he had found the two eunuchs sent into exile by the ex-Khedive. It seems they had sworn to kill Khalil 'Agha, the chief eunuch, but, as their foe had just died a natural death at Suez on his way to Mecca, the exiles would now return to Cairo.

Resuming, the Khedive said, "It is true that I have great power with the people; for instance, the ministers had long been trying to get a certain canal repaired by some villagers, but the villagers disregarded all orders. I sent a telegram, and the thing was done in two days. So, if I tell the people that such or such a thing must not be done, they will obey readily, knowing that I am a good Muslim. If, for example, I order the dervishes to stop the practice of devouring serpents, they will obey me." Seeing a chance here I remarked, "I believe it is true that the people are easily guided by example, and have a great reverence for authority; and this gives Your Highness an enormous power for good. Is it not true then, that if the Khedive tells them that the Dôsah is a wicked practice—cruel, barbarous, and contrary to the religion of Mohammed—the sheikhs will listen to you, and there will be an end of it?"

"Yes," said the Khedive, "it is true; but it is a great deal to ask at present. If I were to forbid the rite now, the people would say I had acted under European pressure, and not of my own free will. But, please God, in a year or two, when the administration is settled and strong, the Dôsah shall end."

Here Turâbi remarked, "Yes, Your Highness, that is right; in a year or two when things are better." Then, turning to me, he added, "Why should it be stopped? it is harmless."

"It is *not* harmless," I replied, sharply; "it is extremely cruel."

There are some facts and stories relating to the slave-trade in Egypt which may be worth putting together here. Much of the information against the authorities came from a certain German whom I could name. All he wrote was quoted in England as gospel; but the Khedive told me that Herr —— had demanded from Riaz Pasha 1000*l*. as the price of his good-will and silence in the matter of slaves. The proposal was flatly rejected; and, failing the hush-money, Herr —— took to humanity.

Evidence of the most certain kind, but such as I cannot in honour quote, proved to me beyond all shadow or colour of a doubt that the Khedive personally is an enemy of slavery. I have said this before; I repeat it. But the same is not true of those about him. When we were up the Nile a certain bey in his service bought a small slave-girl and escaped detection. But one of the Khedive's personal servants who secretly made a similar purchase was discovered; whereupon the Khedive was extremely angry, ordered the man to put the girl ashore, and barely refrained from dismissing him on the spot. During the same voyage a relation of His Highness bought two slave children and managed to conceal them until our return to Cairo. On discovering the fact the Khedive was furious. "What is the use," he said, " of my giving orders to other people, if you set such an example as this?" This scene was related to me by an eye-witness.

The Princess has about sixty maids of honour, tire-women, and the like; but with these the Khedive had nothing to do. He never even looks at them if he can avoid it. Whenever one of them is married, it is customary for him to make a present of two or three negresses, but this custom he has invariably broken.

Once the Khedive told me he had a letter from his agent in Constantinople saying that slaves were continually being sold at Pera, while the British Government fancied slavery abolished in Turkey. The agent even offered to buy a beautiful girl for 300*l.* such as formerly cost 1000*l.* The Khedive sent answer that he had never bought a slave and never would. When I said that it would be extremely difficult to put down the traffic in Egypt while it continued in Turkey, "It will be very difficult," he replied, "but not impossible; it shall be done. My word is pledged to England, and slavery shall cease in Egypt. I have told you now; you will see that my words come true." He spoke with unmistakable earnestness, and added, "I have sent the most stringent orders to the governors of Alexandria, Cairo, and all towns, but especially those on the coast, to suppress all slave-dealing, and I just hear that Riûf Pasha has dismissed the governor of a province in the Sudân for buying a slave boy."

Very low prices were formerly given for slaves. The mother of a certain pasha's children tells that in her own country she was sold for 1*l.*, and another wife relates that she was bartered for a cow. Horrible cruelties are practised on their victims by the dealers. The deep scarred lines that one sees on the faces of many blacks are often cut by the dealers with a knife to imitate the tattoo-marks customary among some of the Sudân tribes; they are a kind of forged hall-mark. A slave-girl in a harim now in Cairo tells how on her passage down the Nile, the boat being surprised at night by a search-party, the slaves were hurriedly thrown overboard with ropes under their arms, and under fearful threats were bidden to keep quiet in the water.

A certain unmentionable pasha once drowned several of his slave-girls and eunuchs together. This happened at a time when the girls were allowed to walk abroad attended by negroes. Various attempts were made to open communication with the girls, and the eunuchs aided by carrying letters. When —— discovered these intrigues, with that cold-blooded brutality characteristic of the man, he ordered all the poor girls and the eunuchs to be bound hand and foot, tied up in sacks, and thrown into the Nile. This story was not only related to me by the present Khedive, but confirmed in every detail by a person who knew many of the fellow-slaves of the murdered girls, and in whose presence one such slave heard the news of the murder, fell ill, and actually died of fright. It was one of ——'s unhappy slave-girls who some years ago set fire to —— Palace, hoping to escape in the confusion. The origin of the fire even now is unknown to the public. At 'Abbasiah there is a kiosk with a well into which —— is said to have had the bodies of his victims thrown, but of this proof is wanting. In a house at Kûbra, however, there is an undoubted *oubliette*, a trapdoor cleverly arranged in the floor of a certain room. This was seen by my informant, and the people of the household all aver that the man who made it used it.

The murder of the Mufettish has already been related, but one night the Khedive told me a good deal more about the man. He had four hundred women-slaves, all gorgeously attired in silks and decked with marvellous jewels. He had a set of twelve golden ash-trays encrusted with brilliants, each little tray worth 500*l.* The kitchen cost 60,000*l.* a year. When the present Khedive (then prince) went with the Princess to pay the Mufettish a visit, they were dumbfounded by the lavish splendour of his palace, which rivalled the richest fancies of the Arabian Nights. When the Mufettish was leaving his palace, his slaves formed a double line from his state-room across the courtyard to the outer gate; as he appeared, all cried aloud, " Behold our lord and master!" And while he moved along all saluted, bowing low, sweeping the right hand downwards and then laying the palm on the top of the head. The Khedive told me a very curious story about the Mufettish's behaviour in his own harim; he had it on the authority of one of his household, who had been intimate with a former slave of the Mufettish, and so had been enabled to peep through an unguarded window. But Herodotus shows clearly that there are some Egyptian stories which ought not to be made known to the vulgar.

But to return to stories of slaves. A few years ago a little girl ten years old was being dragged in chains through the desert with a large gang of slaves. The fatigue and suffering of the march made her so ill that the owner threw her down by the way-side to die, not thinking her worth the trouble of driving further. Seeing this, another dealer remarked, "Are you going to leave the girl?"

"Mâ shâ 'llah, yes; death is written on her forehead."

"Good! then I will take her on the chance of her living."

The girl recovered; but when the gang neared Cairo, the original owner claimed her. Angry words followed. The man who abandoned the little girl swore that he never meant to leave her behind, and, finding that the other would not yield, he turned on the child, and plunged his knife all down her side, thinking to settle the quarrel by killing her. She fell as dead, but the man who had rescued her tended her, and in time once more she recovered. This story was told to me by a lady who had it from the girl's own lips, and who saw the mark of the wound.

Another little girl I heard of, who at the age of four or five years was rescued by Admiral McKillop from a slaver in the Red Sea. She was taken to England, brought up as an English girl, acquired English ways, and knew no other language. An Alexandrian lady met her on board ship, and questioned her to find out how much she remembered of her early life. When asked about her father and mother, the girl without looking up, and without speaking a word, quietly drew her forefinger round her throat.

But, even in 1881, dreadful cruelties were sometimes practised in Cairo. One evening in February, a negress slave escaped, and came to Count Sala to claim her freedom. He referred her to the zaptieh, or police-station; but, when she protested that it was too late to go there, he ordered his bowâb or doorkeeper to give her a room for the night, and to go with her next morning to the zaptieh. Unluckily it was from the house of the officer at that zaptieh that she had run away. Some hours having passed, Count Sala remarked that his bowâb had not returned, and sent to the zaptieh to make inquiries. There the poor man was found lying insensible, with both thumbs shattered, and his feet cut to pieces. When he brought the negress, she was at once accused of larceny and he of complicity; and he was tortured with thumbscrews and kûrbash to make him confess. He was long unconscious, but slowly recovered.

A slave-woman is never liberated if she has stolen anything from her master, or if she fails to show that she possesses means of subsistence. She may therefore always be sent back to slavery on a trumped-up charge of theft.

One Sunday night, talking alone with the Khedive, I showed him Colonel Gordon's recent letter to *The Times* about the slave-trade, and a leader upon it. Both accused the Khedive of not having the convention for the suppression of the traffic published among the natives in Cairo and Upper Egypt, and charged him with insincerity. The fact was true, but the inference wrong; and his failure to publish the agreement was due simply to his dislike of appearing to act under European pressure. He said, "At this moment there is not a slave to be purchased in Cairo; if you wish to buy one, it is impossible. But if I were insincere, and chose to encourage the traffic, or even to connive at it, do you think there would not be hundreds? Colonel Gordon is not like other men, he is above them. The natives here all think him deranged, but certainly even he may be mistaken."

"I see that in this letter," I replied, "Colonel Gordon speaks of the ex-Khedive as 'his friend'; I think that Ismail Pasha would laugh in his sleeve to hear himself quoted as a champion of the abolition of slavery. Undoubtedly he enabled Colonel Gordon to crush the traffic in the Sudân; but what he really liked in Gordon's splendid work was the extension of his empire, the partial fulfilment of his dream of conquest in those regions. I know well that all the time Ismail Pasha was the largest buyer of slaves in Egypt, and the most tyrannical master."

"That is true," said the Khedive; "Gordon was deceived by my father, but liked him nevertheless. Among my father's papers are many curious letters and telegrams from Gordon. Thus, when he dismissed the English and French Controllers, Gordon sent a telegram congratulating him and saying, 'You will be the Sultan.'"

Another point raised in the letter to *The Times* was the retention of Darfûr. The Khedive said he would only too gladly restore the kingdom to one of the Sultan of Darfûr's family; but there were none left now except a boy of twelve, as the unmentionable pasha had had all the rest killed.

I was surprised, but said, "I presume that Your Highness means that they were killed in battle."

"No," he said; "—— had them all murdered in cold blood here in Cairo to the number of eighteen or twenty." So much for the humanitarian.

The measures lately taken for the suppression of the slave-trade by the Khedive's orders had been explained by Dr. Lowe in a letter sent to *The Times* from Cairo; but it was never published. On my remarking upon this fact, the Khedive said quite simply, "Perhaps *The Times* requires bribing." I laughed, and said that was quite impossible. "But I assure you," said the Khedive, "that in my father's accounts there is an item of 10,000*l*. paid to *The Times* for its support." When the Khedive named the agent by whom the bargain was arranged, I could not well doubt that the money had been paid for the alleged purpose, and that it had been intercepted by the agent. In the same accounts sums are entered as paid to nearly all the chief English newspapers as bribes to secure their interest for Ismail, who seems to have been handsomely fooled in the matter.

When Colonel Gordon passed through Egypt on his return journey from India, he sent a telegram from Suez to the Khedive saying. "How is your health and the slave-trade?" But from that date Gordon never came to Egypt again, until Mr. Gladstone sent him forth, and left him to die that death watched by all the world—the most tragic death in history.

Heu pietas! heu prisca fides invictaque bello Dextera.

Speaking of Suez and the Canal, the Khedive added, "The Chief of the 'Ulema, head of all the dervishes in Egypt, is just dead; he was a great fanatic, and once told me that if England treated Egypt badly he would order all his 450,000 men to go to the Suez Canal and fill it up."

Another evening, not long afterwards, the conversation again fell upon Colonel Gordon, and the Khedive repeated that he had discovered among his father's papers many letters and memoranda from

Gordon, one memorandum in particular relative to the Financial Commission. In this the writer advised the then Khedive Ismail, if possible, to refuse the nomination of Mr. Goschen and M. Joubert, or else, when they arrived, to send them about their business. Ismail was not to reject the idea of a Commission of Inquiry, but to inform the Powers that he was quite able to manage it without their assistance. The Khedive assured me that Gordon even went so far as to urge, "You have many soldiers, a very good army; and if needs be you can make war with England and France." As he quoted this statement the Khedive laughed heartily, and said, "I wish all this could be published in *The Times* or *Standard*." After some further discussion, the Khedive said that he and his Government were really and sincerely bent on stopping the trade in slaves, and all the abominations that belong to it.

Many curious stories of native life in Egypt and Turkey followed. I asked whether it was still customary to fling the bodies of inconvenient people into the Bosporus, and the answer was, "Even now, at this day, it is nothing unusual for men to be bowstrung and thrown into the sea."

Some mention has been made of Ismail Pasha; let

me now add a few points to his history. From the accounts, which in the hurry of his departure were left behind, it appears that out of 100,000,000*l.* which he borrowed only about 15,000,000*l.* were spent on public works in Egypt. Concerning the expenditure of the remaining 85,000,000*l.* I shall relate neither what is known to me nor what is unknown. But speaking of his father the present Khedive once said, "There will never be another like him for splendour and magnificence; it is impossible."

I ventured to say, "I think the people need and value good government more than splendour."

"Yes," said Turâbi Bey; "they know that your heart is good towards them and that you study their welfare."

"God knows," was the reply, uttered in a tone of deep earnestness, "God knows that my heart is true towards them; my highest wish is to see them happy and prosperous; there is nothing I care for in comparison."

The opening of the Suez Canal was celebrated by a series of pageants and entertainments on which fabulous sums were lavished. Ismail subsequently had a history of the proceedings published in an elephant folio volume with plates; only three hundred copies were printed, and the cost of the work was 10,000*l.* One copy I possess, a present from the Khedive.

Tewfik had many strange stories of the behaviour of the Empress of the French and other European magnates, but he had nothing but good to say of the Princess of Wales. When the Princess visited Tewfik and his wife there was some conversation about polygamy, and the Princess was astonished to hear Tewfik strongly condemn the system; she was also surprised when he stated that he would never have married a wife unless he loved her. This conversation passed in French, but afterwards the Khedive's mother inquired of him, "What were you talking about all that time?" "Oh," he replied, "the beauties of nature: trees and birds and flowers."

One day the royalties all went for a picnic to Heliopolis, and the whole party, some two hundred in number, rode on donkeys. As they were coming back a group of donkey-boys in the Esbekiah cheered Ismail, who was riding with the Empress. He was quite frightened by the noise, and promptly sent the police, who seized ten of the boys and clapped them into prison. He lived in terror of his life, and would never allow a stranger or a native to come near him if he could avoid it, for fear of a dagger up the sleeve. He had no heart or affection: his sensuality had ruined that. He never kept any of his white slaves very long; it was generally a month or two ere the feeble fancy sputtered out in dull disgust. Occasionally it happens in the harims that a slave proves rebellious, refusing submission; in that case the remedy is brutal coercion—one hundred, or even two hundred, lashes with the bastinado.

"People in Europe," said the Khedive, "would be astonished if they knew Ismail Pasha's real character and history."

"Yes," I said, "he is thought extravagant and selfish, but otherwise polite, clever, and enlightened."

"But," said Tewfik, "please God, those barbarous times are over."

The conversation which closed with this remark was resumed the next evening, when the Khedive told me of his own difficulties under his father's reign. Mr. Vivian at one time had recommended him to take the post of President of the Council of Ministers, but he strongly objected, urging that his father would never give him credit for honest work, but would be eternally suspecting him of plots and cabals. The Prince was overruled, but the result he had foreseen followed, and was subsequently acknowledged by Mr. Vivian in a letter containing only three words—" You were right."

Ismail had Tewfik watched day and night; every action and movement were reported to him by spies, and the name of every visitor chronicled. Tewfik did not condescend to intrigue, and refused all overtures of aid against his father. Thus when he was Regent, during the absence of Ismail on a visit to Europe, he got a letter from a then minister offering him the services of all the land and sea forces, and promising to sink Ismail in the harbour of Alexandria, on his return to Egypt. Tewfik rejected the offer, not once but twice over; but he kept the letters. At the Ceremonies the officials were barely civil to Tewfik, often keeping him waiting two hours before announcing him. Upon his marriage his father would have done nothing but let him marry as a pauper; only here Riaz was firm, and by great exertion arranged for the necessary processions and the full ceremonial for the wedding of a prince and princess. But a minister once said tauntingly to him, " You a prince! Why your father will send you in irons to the Sudán to-morrow if you don't behave." Tewfik answered,

"He is my father and my sovereign, and can fling me into the Nile if he wishes."

Ismail's anger was always roused by the religious tendencies of Tewfik. Once he said to him, "By the head of my father, I will order you to Khartûm, if you play the Musulman like that. What is the use of it? Your interest lies with the Europeans; imitate them; adopt European ways of living and thinking like me. I am not a Musulman; I am a Christian. You will ruin yourself with those fanatic ways of yours." Yet another time, his advice was, "When you come to the throne, pretend to be a good Musulman; the natives will like you for it; it is good policy."

Tewfik lived in daily terror of his life, lest he should be poisoned or otherwise murdered; for the poisoned cup of coffee was an oriental device with which the great men of Egypt were then quite familiar. "I assure you," said the Khedive, "those were dreadful times for me; I can never forget what I suffered. It was only the strength of a good conscience and the resolve to do right that kept me up. Yet I had no personal fear; I did not behave like a coward. And when at last I came to the throne, I received the news without any joy. Sympathy with my father's fall and the great sense of responsibility left no room for rejoicing. My father of course heaped reproaches upon me, and accused me of having intrigued at last successfully. I then produced the letters which the minister had written offering me the army. My father read them, was much moved, and kissed me saying, 'Forgive me, my son, forgive me.' The first day of my accession was a Friday; so I went in state to the mosque. 'What,' said my father, 'still determined to play the Musulman?' 'Yes, sire, more than ever.'"

Ismail's relations with Russia were to say the least curious. Among his papers are many documents showing, that, while he pretended to cultivate the friendship of England and France, he was secretly intriguing with Russia. His idea was that Russia would overthrow Turkey and declare Egypt independent. In the Russo-Turkish war he at first refused to send any troops from Egypt in aid of the Sultan; later when he sent a contingent of 15,000 men, under Hassan Pasha, all were miserably equipped, and the artillery had no horses. In excuse it was alleged that there were no horses then in Egypt, and the Turks had to supply the deficiency. But, even when properly horsed, the artillery, like the rest of the Egyptian contingent, did absolutely nothing. In fact Hassan had secret orders to remain as inactive as possible, and, if he saw an opportunity of secretly damaging the Turkish cause, to seize it and make the most of it. Some will remember Russia's quick declaration that she had no intention of touching Egypt, when Lord Derby warned her off; the above story may help to explain it.

The Khedive told me also that he had seen a letter written by his father to General Ignatieff asking that the Shah of Persia on his visit to Europe should not be allowed to pass through Egypt, and offering the General 6000*l*. to arrange the matter. The reply of General Ignatieff, accepting the offer and stating that the Shah would not pass through Egypt, was also discovered. In this the Khedive could not understand his father's motive.

CHAPTER VIII.

The pyramids in flood-time—Beset by Beduins—Ancient coins—Pistols forgotten—Stories of Arab "saints"—The Mahmal—Festival of Great Bairam—The Chief Eunuch—Visit to Sheikh Mohammed es Sadât—The King's chamber.

ALL travellers to Egypt see the pyramids; few see them in September, when the great valley of the Nile is flooded. Yet at no time is the view of and from the pyramids so impressive; and this must be my apology for touching upon what has become almost a commonplace of travel. It was a hot afternoon towards the end of September when I resolved to make the solitary journey. As the road left Gizah, one found that the great plain, which in winter separates the river from the desert, had become a lake. The causeway stood like a long mole between the waters. On either side there

GROUP OF BEDUINS

spread an almost boundless flood, fringed in the far distance by palm-groves, and checked by the Libyan mountains. Behind one the Mokattem hills rose white and flashing in the sun, yet their outlines half-lost in a mist of burning azure. These far hills, more than any scene I ever beheld, seemed to realise in physical presentment the idea of a golden fairy-land, of a region where lotus-eaters dream away eternal sunshine.

It was a pleasant and cool drive under the long avenue of acacias; for a strong breeze was blowing over the water. I had wished to be alone, but my arrival was noticed, and from the villages the Arab vultures swooped down upon me. They had not had a visitor since the spring to prey upon; now their beaks were whetted and their tongues athirst. It was in vain that I told them that I was no traveller, that I knew the place before they were born, and that it was written on their foreheads they would get no money. They followed in a hungry flock: solitude was impossible: for I had forgotten my revolver, the only thing feared by a Beduin.

So as the less of two evils I chose two men to follow me,—Mohammed and Shahâti; whereupon the rest departed. After a visit to the Sphinx, Mohammed asked me to drink coffee in his house. Descending to the foot of the plateau, I entered the village built of sun-dried bricks, saw the tiny mosque roofed with palm-thatch, and passed within the mud-wall inclosure of Mohammed's dwelling. At the doorway there was a short pause, while a hurry and scurry within announced that the women-folk were withdrawing. We walked across a yard into a sort of shed with open doorway and windows. Half the floor was covered with matting; but for me they spread a handsome rug and a cushion. I reclined at full length, but my repose was brief; for slowly one Beduin after another dropped in, till no less than thirteen were ranged in a circle about me. We talked, and coffee was served, but only one man beside myself was allowed the honour of drinking. Then one by one they brought out their "antikas," blue enamelled figurines, bronzes, stone images, and the like. Most of them were of indifferent interest; others were "under a doubt," and a wave of the hand rejected them. Chaffering was slow work; but as I surveyed the faces round me—some frank and pleasant, others wild and ferocious—I could not help thinking how easily they might rob and murder me in that lonely hut seven miles from Cairo. They knew that I had money about me; I remembered with idle regret that I had no revolver.

But at last one of the Arabs drew forth a bag in which something jingled; he untied the string with his teeth, and slowly rolled out a handful of ancient Greek coins. They looked good; most were familiar to me, and rather fine specimens; but a few I had never seen before. The usual tactics of a deal followed, till I uttered my "last word." The coins were sulkily gathered up, as if to be replaced in the bag; but the Arab, suddenly changing his mind, handed them over to me with an air of cheerful repentance, receiving his money in return. I subsequently found that of the unfamiliar coins two were unique and unpublished, and a third extremely rare; all three are now in the British Museum. They belonged to the region of Cyrene and Barca, and were doubtless brought thence by Arabs passing the pyramids on their way to Cairo; for this is the common route of pilgrims from the northern shores of Africa to Mecca.

I spent a long time in the hut with my Beduin friends, and on coming out enjoyed the view of the Great Pyramid from the village below. From no other point is the view so imposing, for from that low level the eye seems to take in the whole sublimity of the vast fabric towering above. On reascending the plateau I found the sun setting, and I mounted one of the three small pyramids which lie east of the Great Pyramid. Thus the pyramids of Cheops and Chefren formed a framework for the sunset, and their sombre masses showed the luminous space between in admirable clearness, shutting off the light rightward and leftward. Low down on the horizon lay a glow of deep orange colour fading upwards to pale gold and above passing through a mist of amethyst into bright blue; in the blue were floating tiny clouds of deep crimson with umber shadows.

My talk with the Arabs after dinner fell upon the Dôsah; they seemed firmly to believe that the rite served as a test between good and bad dervishes; the latter they said are wounded, the former never suffer. Mohammed told me that he obtained his present wife by paying a sorcerer ten francs. Her father disliked him, and forbade the marriage: but the sorcerer gave Mohammed a paper written with charms, which he buried one night before the threshold of the parents' house, and so true was the spell that in three days the hard heart melted, and the wedding was sanctioned. Some of the Beduins use similar charms to make their guns shoot straight and the shot mortal, while others put no faith in such magic.

Soon after moonrise, which is extremely beautiful at flood-time, I had to leave; and as I walked back to the carriage, Mohammed inquired whether I had pistols. I declined to answer, saying that I might or might not have them. He pressed me further, and I told him to mind his own business. At this he seemed hurt, and said he was only afraid for me, because the Arabs often came out of their villages at night and attacked solitary wayfarers; he himself was assailed the other night when coming home alone, and only his good legs saved him. His manner was impressively earnest, but I declined to admit that there was any reason for alarm. At the carriage I found Shahâti and others, who put the same question about my pistols, got the same answer, and told me dreadful stories of the perils of the route at night. They offered to lend me some of their own weapons, which I refused to take. Just before getting into the carriage, I picked up a large stone to use as a missile in case of need, and so started, not without some uneasiness. Shahâti however refused to leave me, and followed the carriage running on foot. Again and again I told him to go back; he repeated that he was afraid for my life, and ran on beside me. At last seeing his determination, I told him to mount the box, and so we reached Cairo together. No adventure enlivened the way, though Shahâti pointed out many dark and dangerous-looking places among the reeds and trees, where robbers enough might lie in ambush if so minded.

Alighting at Ismailia Palace, I sent the carriage on to 'Abdîn, but the Khedive had gone for a moonlight trip on the water. As I sat in the gardens with Mustapha Pasha, 'Ali Bey, and others, there came up to us the chief eunuch; the whole company rose to salute him except myself, who remained obstinately seated with my back half-turned, taking no notice. Courtiers cringe to him that he may speak well of them in high quarters, but that was one of the points on which I remained at issue with Court custom. It was the same with the *valet-de-chambre*, whose "young woman" I have seen saluted by a Master of the Ceremonies.

Next day I found that the Khedive and pashas were all talking of my lonely visit to the pyramids; all said it was not safe, and I received a solemn caution against such proceedings for the future. What amused me more was to find that my servant on the arrival of the carriage at 'Abdin had carefully lifted out the big stone, which I had forgotten, and had conveyed it to my rooms, where it adorned a table.

"What is this, Mohammed?" I said.

"Mâ shâ 'llah, it is the beautiful antika which your excellency brought in the carriage from the pyramids!"

When in the evening I saw the Khedive, I told him of several pleasant things the Beduins had said about him, and repeated the story of the sorcerer. His Highness told me that the police had now caught a certain notorious fortune-teller, who for the last thirty years in Cairo had played the "holy man," and had traded on his reputation for sanctity to decoy women into his house. After the first interview he would persuade them under promise of great riches and happiness to return arrayed in their best dresses and jewels, cautioning them not to let their husbands or relatives know of the visit on pain of spoiling the charm and reaping terrible curses. He then murdered and robbed them. The Khedive said that in this way he had killed no less than one hundred women, and contradicted Turábi, who thought the number exaggerated. The saint confessed to five murders of the kind; he was justly hanged.

Ten years ago there was another "holy man," who won great fame by his solitary ascetic life and miraculous gift of healing. He lived in a cave in the desert, and the special charm he exercised was for the cure of barrenness. Many women resorted to him in secret, and after going through certain rites in his cell returned with a charm which in due time was effectual. But one day Osman Pasha (now governor of Siût), and some other officers, hearing strange stories of the recluse's virtues and powers, determined to pay him a visit. They found him in the cave, shrouded in a religious gloom, which entirely concealed his features. But, desiring to know what manner of man he was in the flesh who had so great spiritual power, they kindled torches; and as the flames lit up the cavern, they beheld in the saint a burly muscular sergeant who had deserted from their own regiment. They seized him and bound him and took him to the barracks, where they gave him five hundred lashes, which cured his sanctity.

Yet another saint of the same feather now lives in the Arab quarter of Cairo near the fish-market. He pretends to great virtues, and practises all vices. None but women are received by him, and he leads captive their silly imaginations by mumbling texts and telling his beads, as he promises them all the wealth and splendour of the East. He lives in filth and squalor, his hair and nails unshorn, and his body clothed only by vermin; yet he tells his visitors that he knows the future, that he is a friend of God and talks with God, that he can give riches and honour to whom he pleases. They, poor souls, take it all for gospel, and in the fervour of their faith refuse him nothing.

It was towards the end of September that the departure of the Mahmal took place — a sort of howdah containing the sacred carpet annually sent in solemn procession to Mecca by the Khedive. The start is from the square below the citadel, which from an early hour was thronged by troops, while all the points of vantage, the slopes under the walls, the gateway, ramparts, balconies, and minarets, were occupied by sightseers. The white or blue dresses of the women and the many-hued raiment of the men shining in a strong sunlight made a scene very picturesque and quite oriental. In the spring, when the Mahmal returns, the crowd is half European;

now there were only six Europeans present. The Khedive arrived at 8·30 a.m., and alighted at the tent of crimson silk prepared for him, while the citadel artillery thundered a salute. Then a procession of camels, forming at the far side of the square, advanced to an open space before the tent. There they circled three times round; the Mahmal camel was led forward to the tent, and the sheikh handed the tasseled camel-rope to the Khedive, who at once delivered it to the chief officer of the guard, in token that he was to watch over the Mahmal during the journey, and render it safe and sound on his return to Cairo. The officer when he reaches Cairo again delivers up the tassel to the Khedive with like ceremony.

The procession now moved on. First came a long escort of lancers and carabineers, then torchbearers with their portfire shrouded in coloured silk, then six men riding horses and wearing robes of cream-coloured silk embroidered in places with red chequer designs. These were the men appointed for the service of the camels. After them came a company of singers on foot, carrying long staves; a number of mounted officers; two men swinging censers of burning incense; then the Mahmal—a red silk canopy, gold-embroidered, with poles at each corner surmounted by inlaid silver globes and crescents, and a similar ornament on the summit. The camel which carries the Mahmal has gorgeous trappings, cloth of gold on his head, and a plume of ostrich feathers on his nose. The Amir el Haj, or Prince of the Pilgrims, rides on a second camel decked with small flags, and from his saddle hang various chattels including a large handbell. The third camel bears a wild-looking man called Sheikh of the Camels, a corpulent figure, long-haired and bearded, naked down to the waist, and bareheaded Another camel is ridden by the Sheikh of the Cat, whose charge according to ancient custom is a grimalkin chosen to perform the pilgrimage. Whether this custom is a relic of the old Egyptian cat-worship or not, I can only conjecture. A Sheikh of the Banner, six camels with musicians, and five with pilgrims, followed: some of these were adorned with large tufts of palm-leaves rising like huge plumes from the saddle: and last of all came a single camel bearing a capacious box of provisions slung on either side. The procession is followed out of the city by dervishes bearing the insignia of their various orders, some in sham armour, some with knives or serpents, some carrying poles on which are hung gauze nets enclosing fishes. A guard of cavalry two hundred strong goes with the pilgrims to Mecca, the officers most picturesquely arrayed in purple and gold and scarlet uniforms, riding on high-backed saddles covered with cloth of gold, and wearing silver-hilted scimetars.

Not long after the departure of the Mahmal the chief of all the dervishes, Said el Bekri, died. The dervishes form a corporation or brotherhood linked together by a kind of freemasonry. They are not recognised by the Mohammedan religion, though their ties are mainly religious. Their chief is appointed by the ruler of Egypt, who in this case chose the son of the deceased. His investiture took place at Ismailia Palace with great ceremony. Towards noon a vast procession of dervishes came through the streets bearing great banners. These banners are hung on poles about fifteen feet long; a few are plain, but most are parti-coloured, red, green, black, and yellow, decked with conventional borders, and flowers, and texts from the Korân in *appliqué* work. The poles are surmounted by globes or crescents or pierced designs in silver or bronze. As the procession reached the palace, the men took up positions along the road outside, and a turbaned throng soon blocked the space between the two long lines of dervishes. Not a sound broke the solemn stillness peculiar to an oriental crowd—that hush which contrasts with the roar and surge of an English crowd, much as the silence of a palm-grove in spring contrasts with the " wild music" that " burthens every bough " in an English woodland. Soon a bustle was heard outside; but it was only a pair of oxen dragging a heavy load on one of the low sideless wains of the country, and forcing a slow passage through the mob. Another stir, yet without any murmur of voices, and this time it was the sheikh and his escort. He entered the palace walls, and was taken to an ante-room. When the Khedive was ready, the sheikh and his attendants advanced across the gardens to the marble terrace. Thence he ascended the steps to the vestibule, while his followers stood in a group below, their splendid silk raiment thrown into brilliant relief upon the white marble background. Their outer robes or " gibbahs " were each of a single colour, black, brown, and sea-green, violet and azure, scarlet and crimson; beneath, the striped " kaftan " was of a colour to match the gibbah. The turbans were mostly white, of the form called "muklah"; but the sons of the Prophet wore green as usual. As a study in dress and colour the scene was matchless.

Meanwhile within the Khedive greeted the new sheikh, and pointed him to a divan. Coffee was brought in gold holders, and the state-pipe with jewelled stem. The Khedive talked and advised the chief, and requested him gradually to suppress all such religious practices as were contrary to humanity, such as the Dôsah, serpent-eating, and self-mutilation; and the sheikh promised acquiescence. Then the robe of office was brought, a dark green silk gown trimmed with sable, and the sacred turban, which is nearly two feet in diameter. It consists of a huge black scarf wound round and round a green cap in compact folds. The cap is declared to be seven hundred years old— only the outer covering has been renewed from time to time. But, when the turban was set upon his head and the robe about his shoulders, the sheikh, who had long been combating his emotion, now turned white and faint. Water was given him in vain; he had to be supported and rather dragged than led in a collapsed state down the marble stairs, where a splendid grey Arab charger, the gift of the Khedive, was waiting to carry him away. The bridle was hung with fringes and tassels, and a long tasseled fringe hung over the horse's chest; the raised pommel and back of the saddle were overlaid with brasswork chased in designs of flowers; the broad stirrups also were of chased brass; the saddle-cover and the saddle-cloth were of green velvet embroidered with gold thread. The sheikh was lifted up into the saddle and held there by his followers, who grasped his legs on either side; and as he moved away one went before him singing verses of the Korân. At the palace gate the chief bowed fainting over the neck of his horse, and again was plied with water. As he revived, the charger began to kick and plunge at sight of the forest of flags without. But at last all was ready; the attendant sheikhs mounted their Arabs, which were sumptuously caparisoned and carried each a rich prayer-carpet in place of the saddle-cloth; the banners swayed and moved forward; and the whole procession re-formed to pass through the streets of the city.

Soon after this Cairo was visited by an epidemic of dengue fever. Scarcely any one escaped it, and when my turn came my Berber servant, whom I had tended through it, showed his gratitude by deserting me. When I recovered, the Khedive told me that Mohammed 'Ali Bey, my pupil, was ill with it, and the nurse refused to allow him to take the doctor's prescriptions, but killed a chicken and poured the blood down the little fellow's back, as a charm better than all drugs. Of course the Khedive was very angry, and ordered her dismissal. One result of the epidemic was to frighten away travellers, and among them General Roberts, returning home from his victories in Afghanistan. But though painful at the time—called, in fact, the " bone-breaker "— dengue fever is seldom dangerous, and seldom leaves any evil seeds behind it.

By the festival of the Great Bairam, Cairo had recovered. Muslims tell of the origin of this festival that the Prophet used to have a set time for exchanging visits with his friends, and that the practice became consecrated into a rite by his followers; they also amalgamated with it the custom of annual sacrifice, which had existed in the East from time immemorial, and which is still regarded by the Arabs as a commemoration of Isaac's deliverance from death at the hands of Abraham. On the first of the four days of the Great Bairam, young buffaloes are slaughtered and their flesh is given to the poor. Moreover, every Muslim house offers up the sacrifice of a sheep; rich men sacrifice several; and the ignorant among them believe that for every sheep they kill they will be rewarded with a houri in

Paradise. This is their manner of laying up treasure in heaven.

An hour after sunrise the music of the national air awoke me, and I found the square of 'Abdin lined with soldiers and the Khedive coming in state. First rode the Master of the Horse on a black Arab, and behind him six Turkish fore-riders prancing and curveting their horses. Their uniform of blue and gold, with flying sleeves, broad sashes, scarlet pantaloons, and embroidered gaiters, was most gorgeous. An open carriage followed, drawn by four greys, and containing the Khedive, Riaz Pasha, and another minister. Saices ran alongside in their flowing white tunics and vests of rich needlework; and the Vice-regal guardsmen brought up the rear. After a brief visit to the mosque, the Khedive entered the palace, and at once held the customary *levée*.

When it was over, I paid a visit to H.H. the Princess, who of course does not appear on the scene. One is received by the chief eunuch, who points to a book where the visitor writes his name. All round the reception-room were beys and pashas glittering with gold; and one of them, 'Ali Bey, insisted on my going through the Muslim form of embracement, which on this day varies the everlasting shaking of hands. The chief eunuch was most gracious—a fact which amused me, as only a week previously I had ordered him out of that very room. I had been there at work with the princes, when the eunuch entered without permission. I at once determined that he should depart: so I called my friend 'Ali Bey, and said,

"The Khedive's orders are that no one enters this room while I am engaged with the princes."

He replied, "That is written on the cucumber-leaf, O sir: but there is no one here."

"No one here? then what is that on the divan yonder?"

At once his face became alarmed; his alarm doubled as I said, "Please tell that man to go."

"Bismillah," said 'Ali, "you forget that he is a great person. His Highness's chief eunuch! Never mind to-day. Let us be quiet to-day. Please God, you can speak to-morrow, to-morrow."

Seeing that I could get no help from 'Ali, I walked up to the eunuch, who rose and saluted. I repeated the Khedive's order; he remained silent and standing. I turned to 'Ali Bey and said, "If this man remains, the lesson is over." Then, seeing the eunuch still there, I shut up the books, saying, "We have finished," and took the princes away. As we were leaving the room, 'Ali Bey screened himself a moment behind the *portière*, and with a merry twinkle in his eyes whispered, "Bravo, bravo, bravo!" laying great emphasis on the last syllable. He waited till I had taken the princes in, and on my return almost danced for joy as he exclaimed,

"Splendid! Admirable! God lengthen your life for this!"

I replied, "Everybody is afraid of that man: I am not. I regard only the Khedive's order." So closed the incident, which is a curious illustration of oriental character.

But to resume. Though the Princess does not see any but ladies, she holds her own reception at the Bairam, and is attired in her most splendid jewels. On this occasion she wore a large coronet of diamonds rising in five points, a necklace of diamonds with a marvellous pendant, and a diamond star on the left breast. Her fingers were ablaze with jewels, among which was a brilliant as large as a filbert. The maids-in-waiting were dressed in silks of every colour, bound with a sash round the waist; their trains gathered up and fastened at the knees in front in some strange fashion. Receptions were also held by the Prince Mahmûd and Ibrahim Pasha at their own palaces: indeed, one had to spend the day in a round of palaces.

Among rich people at the Bairam there is much giving and receiving of presents. In the days of Ismail every one at the Court was presented with a gift—a sword, a horse, or a costly jewel. Turâbi told me that he once saw twenty trays full of jewels destined as largess for the courtiers. Those days are over.

The processions which convey the presents of a wealthy pasha are curious, generally moving in two single files with an open space between them. First comes a band of music; then six men, in court dress and white gloves, carrying in each hand a long candle swathed in muslin; behind these follow a dozen men dressed in native costumes of crimson silk, each bearing on his white-turbaned head a round tray, overlaid with silver gauze. Under the gauze one may see dishes of sweetmeats and various little boxes and parcels done up in silk. Sometimes the procession is formed of carriages, each tray-bearer sitting alone in solemn state with his tray upon his knees. If close carriages follow, they contain ladies who are about to pay a visit, and whose presents thus go before them.

Similar trays of presents are seen on the occasion of a marriage, when it is usual for the bridegroom to entertain his acquaintances. Here again the English custom is reversed—the bridegroom receives nothing, but gives wedding-presents to all his friends. He is doubtless too happy to question from the giver's point of view the value of indiscriminate charity. Contrary to the statement of Lane, or perhaps owing to a change of usage, the signature of a marriage contract is now customary. When, for example, I was invited to Yakûb Bey's wedding, the guests assembled at his house in the morning and witnessed the signature: the presents were handed round: and the company dispersed to meet again at the dinner-hour, and to see the torchlight procession of the bridegroom returning from the mosque.

Though the Bairam is the great season of rejoicing, it seems to follow immediately upon a season of mourning. That, however, is left to the women. On the eve of the festival, as I was riding in the desert past the great place of sepulture that lies to the south of Cairo, I found most of the recent tombs surrounded by groups of women, who sat on the ground crying, and shrieking, and wailing as they are depicted on ancient monuments. On every side was lamentation, and mourning, and woe. Many of the mourners had decked the tombs of their lost friends with flowers and palm-branches; some had pitched a tent actually over the tomb, so that they might sit in shelter, eat, sleep, and mourn uninterruptedly. But the smoking fires and simmering vessels upon them showed that fasting is not part of the ceremonial.

About this time I had the honour of an invitation to visit the courtly and genial Sheikh Ahmed Mohammed es Sadât, who dwells in one of the few ancient palaces of Cairo now remaining. His family is said to have lived in the same house for eight hundred years, which might be true if the house were four or five hundred years older. I drove, accompanied by an orderly, through the narrow winding streets, and after a brisk but harmless collision with another carriage arrived before the portal. There six servants rose in salute and led me into the courtyard, where the sheikh was seated in splendid robes on a curious antique bench. His smiling face beamed the welcome, which his lips uttered with oriental effusiveness as he rose and took me by the arm to show me about. First we went to the great reception room, a beautiful hall sixty feet long and forty feet high; three large bays on either side vary the width. The hall is paved with marble, and is divided in the middle into two levels by a step; all round the dais or upper level runs a divan against the wall, and the light comes in from lofty windows, but the other half of the building is lighted only by a large cupola or lantern above. In the western wall is a fountain-head which shoots a stream of water into a marble basin. Every inch of the basin was originally covered with Damascus and Rhodian tiles of most splendid designs; but now in many places these have fallen, and are still falling, and where they are gone they are replaced by plaster frescoed into a rude resemblance of the ancient patterns. All round the dais, however, the tile-work is still perfect. The roof is of woodwork most exquisitely gilt and coloured, and the main beams rest on stone corbels ornamented with graceful stalactite carving; but the corbels as well as the spandrels above are painted and touched with gilt to match the ceiling.

Here we rested to drink the indispensable smoke and coffee—for an Egyptian does not "smoke tobacco" but "drinks smoke"; then Ahmed took me to see his "study," a long low room with a finely-carved ceiling, and windows opening on to a garden.

Here books, reed-pens, and papers were lying about, mostly on the rich carpets of the floor: there was no seat except divans, and of course no writing-table; for the Arabs always write upon the palm of the left hand, as did the ancient Egyptians. A third room was reached by passing under a long arcade of vines, and displayed another splendid roof and a marble floor finely inlaid with mosaic. The mushrabiahs, or lattice-windows, of the harîm above are some of the finest in Cairo, and through them are caught dim glimpses of other wonderful chambers; but the ladies were there, and entrance was of course forbidden. So, after a glance at the private mosque, I took my leave, and was escorted to the carriage by my host, who overwhelmed me with salâms and polite farewells.

Another celebrity whom I met one evening at a native dinner was also called Sheikh Mohammed, a young poet of great renown. Musicians sat cross-legged on benches singing his songs to the 'aûd, kanûn, kamanga, and tambourine. Here in the East the poet is necessarily himself a musician. He writes the words of his song, and sets it to music; then he sends for the players, sings to them, and teaches them the words and accompaniment. These musicians teach others, and so the song is published. Thus doubtless were published the ballads of Homer and songs of Anacreon. On the night I write of Sheikh Mohammed wore a lavender silk robe with a yellow striped kaftan beneath, carried a long, ivory-headed wand, and was very drunk.

Egyptian clocks always strike the hour twice over, waiting a minute between whiles. For, as a native said to me, the first time one is generally asleep; and, if one happens to be awakened by the noise, one does not hear the full number told. To get up and see the time, or even to open the eyes needlessly, is fatiguing: therefore the clock begins over again. Perhaps on something the same principle I may recount another visit to the pyramids, which took place about a month after that related at the beginning of this chapter; yet it shall not be a mere repetition. For on this occasion, just as we reached the desert, rain began to fall—the first since eight months ago—and the sky was overcast with a leaden gloom worthy of an English November. The result was to give the pyramids a look of the most sombre and terrible melancholy, such as those who have only seen them under the brilliance of sun or stars can not well imagine. The colour of the stone was deepened in the rain; the landscape around was darkened; the Sphinx wore its eternal smile, yet looked draggled and unhappy; for its eyes could not see the eastern hills in front. A sense of indignity, of glory departed, was over the whole scene. Certainly in a cloudy climate the pyramids would be unbearable.

A faint rose glow at sundown gave hopes of a fair evening, but after hoping in vain we resolved at last to retire for shelter into the interior of the Great Pyramid. The downward shaft from the entrance was naturally very wet; but, once at the bottom, we mounted in drought and heat the long sloping corridor which leads to the king's chamber. Candles were soon burning and rugs spread, but the darkness was so intense that our six lights only availed to illumine one end of the chamber. We dined with six Arabs waiting upon us, and towards the end of dinner there silently entered a seventh—a very fine old man—who carried a brazier of burning charcoal. He took not the least notice of any one present, but set down his brazier at the far end of the chamber, and put upon the coals a small ewer of brass. Then he sat, or rather squatted, before the fire, singing a wild monotonous song or incantation, only stopping a moment now and then to blow upon the embers.

As his breath fanned the coals into a bright glow, a red reflection was cast on his dark profile and grizzled beard, his bronzed and sinewy arms bared to the shoulder, his white robe and snowy turban; and, when he ceased breathing on the fire, the reflection faded into the gloom. It was like some scene in an enchanter's cavern, as one watched his complete absorption in his work, his unconsciousness of any human presence, and his strange figure, as he sang half-invisible over his dull embers, then flashed into bright relief.

But the potion distilled in the alembic of our magician was merely coffee, and very good it proved; it is a pity that westerns are unskilled in such alchemy. We sat smoking and talking some time; then, as the rain was still falling outside, the Arabs entertained us with songs and dances, which pleased them, but savoured perhaps of irreverence in such surroundings. But waiting was useless, and we returned in pouring rain under a moonless sky.

CHAPTER IX.

Black arts—Khedive and magician—A Coptic dealer in charms—Remarkable Persian ceremony—Sanguinary rites—Litany and lections—More talk about the Dôsah—Arab myths.

STORIES of oriental magic have always their own fascination. One is half inclined to credit wise men of the East with possessing a tradition of occult science long lost among the restless changes of the West. Such a story now came under my notice. The Khedive sent for me one evening, and said:

"I have something curious to tell you. There is a Turk here in Cairo who wears a ring which he pretends is gifted with magic virtues. I have seen him and the ring—it is a plain hoop of gold set with a red stone, which is said to have come from Mecca. The Turk also showed me a plate of silver engraved with verses from the Korân. He explained that he could not work the charm himself, but required a child under ten years of age. The child takes the ring, the silver plate is put on his head, and in a little while the colour of the stone changes to white. Thereupon the child looks into the stone, and sees in it visions, and can answer any questions."

The Khedive went on to say, that, being quite incredulous, he asked for permission to take the ring home, and try it in private. The owner consented. So the Khedive took the ring to Ismailia Palace, where there happened to be a little girl eight years old belonging to the nurse—an ignorant child, unable to read or write. When the plate of silver was laid on her head, and the ring given into her hand, almost immediately she cried out, "The stone has turned to white." The Khedive then asked questions about persons whom the child had not seen, and received correct descriptions. Another person present asked:

"How many children have I?"

"Two sons and a daughter."

"That is right. What is the elder son like?"

"He wears a coat with a row of buttons down the front, and striped trowsers, and has a sabre."

"What is the second son like?"

"He has a coat with two rows of buttons in front,

little gold cushions on his shoulders, and an anchor embroidered on his cuffs."

The one was in the Turkish army, the other in the Turkish navy, and both were absolutely unknown to the child. Collusion was impossible; for even a wizard would find it hard to penetrate into the ladies' apartments of the Khedive's palace. Moreover the questions were too rapid and too varied to admit of shuffling or guessing answers. The Khedive's conclusion was: "I cannot believe it, and yet I cannot understand it."

After some talk about English mesmerists and clairvoyants, the Khedive related that once, before he came to the throne, he consulted a soothsayer in company with the Minister of War.

"What is the news for Egypt?" he asked.

The soothsayer demanded two minutes delay, and then replied, "War with Abyssinia."

"Will the Egyptian army conquer?"

"Give me six minutes," replied the sorcerer.

At the end of that time his face became very troubled, his voice faltered, and his whole body shook, as he answered, "The Egyptians will be defeated, and their army destroyed; only a small remnant shall be left." The prince laughed at the prophecy, and forgot it; but two months later the same Minister of War showed him a despatch from Upper Egypt, stating that the army had been utterly routed, and four battalions out of six annihilated. After showing the despatch, the minister remarked, "Do you remember our friend the sorcerer?" and the prince recollected. Now as Khedive he regards the thing as a curious coincidence.

Here Tonino Bey entered, and gave an account of his meeting Major Baring at the station, and welcoming him in the Khedive's name. The Khedive invited him to remain, and re-told to him in French the story of the ring; I thus heard it twice over, and the two versions tallied exactly. Before I left, the Khedive promised that he would try to get the ring again, and that I should witness some experiments.

A few days later, His Highness told me that he had seen the man with the ring, and asked to borrow it again, but the man became suspicious and alarmed. One of the pashas at the Court had offered him 100*l.* for the ring, which was one hundred times its intrinsic value, but the offer was rejected. At the Khedive's second demand the magician was thoroughly frightened, thinking he should never see his treasure again, and, bursting into tears, he implored the Khedive not to take it away. Thereupon the Khedive said:

"You are mistaken in thinking that I believe in the powers of your ring, or in things of the kind. I wish you good morning." The man's name was Ahmed 'Agha; but, though I hunted Cairo over, I could find no trace of him; he was probably scared away from the city. But I learnt another curious thing about him. The people said that he had cured many sufferers of rheumatism by thrusting needles into their legs, and neck, or shoulders. No blood was let by the process, and no pain inflicted.

In Lane's "Modern Egyptians"* there is a curious tale of divination, as practised by means of a mirror of ink. The facts are given partly on the writer's own authority, and, if true, are remarkable enough. I believe, however, that Lane acknowledged having been deluded in the matter. I made diligent inquiries in Cairo for any magician who could divine by the magic mirror, and promised to give him a handsome largess; I also promised a reward to any native who would find me such a person. But in vain. The answer came back in three or four days that

* Vol. i. ch. 12.

there was no such man in Cairo, and that nobody had ever heard of one living.

Dealers in charms are of course common enough, their reputation depending only on the credulity of their customers. One such dealer was an aged Copt, a very eccentric character, and one of the most learned men of his community. The charms, which he wrote on slips of parchment, were Bible texts in the ancient Coptic language, and these he gave to his fellow-Christians. But such was his fame that Muslim men and women came and besought his aid. To a Muslim he would say:

"Here, my friend, take this text; it is one that suits your case exactly. Wear it upon your heart by day, and place it under your pillow by night." The suppliant departed with a sense of relief and hope, quite unaware that the Coptic text, if interpreted, meant, "Mohammed is in hell-fire." In truth the Copt was much too enlightened to believe in the charms, though they pleased his sense of humour. But his poor mother had great faith in them, and when her son fell ill, she sought out his best amulets, and laid them secretly under his pillow in pathetic anxiety.

But, though disappointed in the search after magicians, I saw at this time a sight as unknown in Europe as it is revolting. All over the East the Persians celebrate with bloody rites of their own the anniversary of the death of Hosain, the Prophet's grandson, who was slain on the plain of Karbalah; but nowhere is the ceremony performed with more fanatic zeal than in Cairo. There, on the evening of the tenth day of the first Mohammedan month, prayers are held in the mosque of Hasanain, and subsequently a procession of men, clad in white, cutting themselves with swords and knives, passes through the streets to the house of the chief Persian in the city, where the rites are completed. Many people see the procession, but no Europeans are admitted to the house. By exceptional fortune, however, or rather thanks to the Khedive's kindness, I received a special invitation, and went, accompanied by an orderly and an officer of the ceremonies, to the residence of the great Persian on the evening of the festival.

Formerly in the daytime the mosque of Hasanain was the scene of various solemnities, as described by Lane; but, now that the mosque has been rebuilt in a wretched sham-gothic style, the fear of dirt and disorder has caused the old ceremonies to be abolished.

And there was no great stir in the streets. A little child came up to me, and said, "In the name of the Prophet give me a new year's gift," and a crowd of water-carriers beset me with the same request; but nothing more happened until we reached the Persian consul's house soon after sunset.

Passing across the courtyard we were shown upstairs, and regaled with coffee and cigarettes by our host. Below we could see the courtyard draped in black; it was roofed over with a large awning, and hung with lanterns. A pulpit also, shrouded in dark green cloth, was erected against one wall, and on the pulpit-steps many tapers were burning, as well as two large candles in lofty silver candlesticks. Slowly the courtyard filled with Persian figures: and ladies in balloons of silk, with closely-veiled faces, flitted across and vanished upstairs into the harim. Our room, too, began to receive the more honoured guests.

Four long hours we had to wait, and no signs of procession or of dinner. It was just nine o'clock when our host rose from a grave and silent company and bade us to supper. We found a long table laid in a fine room with a beautifully panelled and painted ceiling. Our food was rice—set in large bowls, and prepared in various savoury methods,—lentils, a sort of cold stewed meat, and a tasteless jelly. It was a real Persian dinner, very good of its kind, and a feast to our fasting palates. Each person had a fork, but the Persians preferred their fingers. One of the guests amused me by his method of eating, which was as follows: taking a plateful of rice he poured oil over it, blended it together, then seized a handful, which he kneaded into a solid ball as large as his mouth would hold. He thrust it home with his fist, and repeated the process *ad satietatem*.

Not less interesting was another Persian, who sat opposite me on a divan smoking as we supped. I never before or since saw the ideal of an imperturbable oriental so perfectly realised. There he sat cross-legged, his robe laid over his feet, his head encircled by an immense turban, his left arm reclining on the side of the divan to hold his cigarette, which he smoked with such long deliberate tranquillity that neither hand nor lip was ever seen moving. His fine open eyes were fixed immoveably before him, yet seemed always to meet one's glance with a bright yet dreamy expression. When we rose from the table his eyes never changed; he saw and cared for nothing about him, but sat like the monarch of a world of shadows. He did not join us again, but probably remained all the evening in the same position, gravely unconscious: and for all I know may be there still.

Only eight guests were at table; and when the meal was over, all returned to the reception-room; but as this was twenty feet above the courtyard, I went down with an Egyptian friend, and was placed in a seat of honour on a raised dais close by the pulpit. A nargileh was brought, and we were soon puffing away as calmly as if we had met, unconscious of any coming excitement, solely to dream over the tranquil fumes of tobacco. During the whole evening two Arab sheikhs had been chanting verses from the Korân; and the greater of the two, Sheikh 'Ali, was sitting so close in front of me now that my knees touched his portly shoulders. When his turn came to sing again, he chose a pinch of snuff, and, retaining it between his finger and thumb, first swayed his great head, then rocked and rolled his enormous body with ponderous balance; and so, first humming a stave, he lifted up his voice and cried with that mixture of drawl and screech which the Arabs call singing. At every pause the crowd shouted, "Allah!

Allah!" and the sheikh whisked his snuff-laden fingers so swiftly across his nose that the one pinch lasted for twenty applications.

During this song the procession had been coming from the mosque. And now a woman descending from the harim passed out into the street, and quickly returned with a man, who carried in his arms a child bleeding and screaming. Both disappeared upstairs. The child—who had represented Hassan, the brother of Hosain, in the procession—had been cut and wounded by his father, though not severely.

Soon messengers came running in to announce the coming of the procession: a noise of shouting gathers outside and grows louder and louder; the doors are hastily flung open, and three tall banners advance, and men with flaming cressets round them. The noise is now very near; a deep, guttural howling like that of a host of angry madmen, changing sometimes to a frenzied yelling, and mingled with the metallic clash of swords. A white horse with a long white saddle-cloth enters; a little boy clothed in white is riding him, and carrying a small scimetar, while the blood flows over his cape from some shallow gashes on his head. The trappings of the horse, too, have been dyed with a rude design in blood. The child represents Hosain, and seems calm and quiet, as if his wounds did not trouble him. When the horse reached the middle of the court, he was wheeled round to face the east, and all the people shouted.

The clamour reached the gates, and we all stood up in intense expectation, as through the doorway came pouring in wild disorder some five-and-twenty wild-looking men, waving curved scimetars and brandishing long knives, with gestures of the maddest excitement; while their shaven heads were hacked with wounds, from which blood was streaming all over their white linen robes. It was like a charge of fanatics flushed with blood in battle: they seemed as if ready to hack themselves or each other to pieces: and, though I was the only European in the courtyard, I could not but feel that the slightest impulse might turn their fury even on the friendly crowd around. Nothing, I thought, could better give one the idea of actual battle; though strangely enough one felt none of the horror with which one imagines such scenes. But, after rushing pell-mell together and clashing their weapons furiously in the middle of the yard, the men were formed into a sort of ring round the boy on horseback, who still faced the east; there they shook their swords above their heads, and continued to wound themselves as they shouted, or rather howled, in deep savage tones, "Hassan! Hosain!"

In this ring they rushed twice round, brandishing their knives and hacking their faces. Then the horse was led away, and disappeared through the staircase doorway, and I had leisure to observe them. Their eyes were afire with excitement. Their heads were shaven in various ways, most with a lane mown from the forehead to the crown through the hair, others with the crown quite bald, and some with just a tuft of long hair left hanging at the extreme back of the head. Their wounds were chiefly on the top of the head, and not as a rule serious; but only in one case did I suspect a man of having borrowed blood; and some had great gaping gashes laying open the whole cheek, and the clotted blood stood out an inch thick. Two or three men moved about inside the ring, mopping the wounds; the white dresses were dyed with splashes and streams of crimson, and some men had large parts of their robes soaked in blood. It was a ghastly but fascinating spectacle. The shouts continued, and the momentary lull was followed by a fresh outburst, as another party entered with two riderless horses, each caparisoned in white and carrying on his back a helmet and suit of ancient mail.

These two horses were led straight across the courtyard through the throng and disappeared at once.

Now the attendants tried to stop the barbarous sword-dance; some gave up their weapons peaceably, from others they were wrenched and wrested by main force. Then, each man holding his neighbour in front by the girdle, they all rushed and plunged forward, and vanished through the same doorway as the horses before. Then men came and gathered up the curved scimetars and broad double-edged knives and daggers, which had been flung, dripping, in a heap on the floor, and carried them away by the armful. These swordsmen who mutilated themselves were dervishes. In the house they took off their white robes, and those who were not too badly wounded returned and mingled in the crowd, with a calm bearing which showed that they were not worked upon by hashish or any other drug. Throughout the rest of the ceremony they were only distinguished by their blood-stained turbans; but, as far as I could judge, only eight or ten of the whole number reappeared.

The next scene in the drama was the recital in Persian of a solemn litany in memory of the two martyrs. A sheikh stood at the foot of the draped staircase on the platform, and intoned slowly, in a fine clear voice, a very musical chant. At the end of every verse came a refrain or chorus, which was caught up by the crowd in the centre of the court-yard—that is, almost exclusively people who had taken part in the procession. While they sang the chorus—

"Hosain! Ah! —— Hosain! Ah! —— Ah! Hosain!"

they beat their breasts furiously. Some few were stripped to the waist and smote both breasts; but most merely opened their robes, and beat the left breast with the right hand. They struck with the open palm really savage blows, that resounded with a loud sharp clap, and after striking they flung back the hand outwards to its farthest reach, to bring it home again with the greatest force. And in the midst of all were three stalwart men of negro race, naked to the waist, who wielded scourges made of chains tipped with leather. These men, as the others beat their breast, raised high their scourges in both hands, and, in accompaniment to the refrain, lashed themselves on either shoulder-blade alternately with rapid swing from stroke to stroke. The noise of the rattling chains and the hard thumps, as the blows descended on their bare flesh with a force that seemed enough to crush the bones, was barbarously revolting. One saw, however, no worse result than an ugly flush under their dark skins; there was no blood let.

All the Persians present joined with various degrees of enthusiasm in the refrain, most merely patting the left breast in rhythm without removing the robe; but all wore a look of intense solemnity. During the whole evening I never saw a single glance cast upwards to the harim, though there one spied plainly enough through the Venetian shutters some beautiful faces unveiled, and looking down on the ceremony. When the litany was ended, the men with scourges and the other half-naked men began to belabour themselves more furiously than ever, till at last they were forcibly stopped, and sent away indoors to clothe themselves.

Next there followed a prose recital of the story of Hosain's death in Persian. A sheikh mounted the pulpit stairs, and sat down upon the topmost step between the banners. In a fine, ringing, impressive voice he told the tale. The audience were now seated on the ground and on the benches, their eyes all fixed intently on the speaker. At the more pathetic parts they cried and sobbed like children, and beat their foreheads for grief. There was nothing like sham or affectation in it; old men and young men and boys wept in their handkerchiefs, whimpered like babies, or shook through all their frame in agony of sorrow. It was very astonishing to witness the passionate personal heart-broken anguish with which men, whom one knew familiarly as quiet industrious workers in brass, calm polite carpet-merchants, or wary dealers in antiques, were affected as they listened to the story of a youth slain in battle twelve centuries ago. It showed an unsuspected capacity for passion in oriental character, and it set one thinking on parallels in our own religion and in mythology.

When the recital in Persian was finished, another man mounted in place of the narrator, and retold the story in Arabic. This was followed with the same fervid sympathy, and the same expression of hopeless mourning.

The Arabic recital was as a rule slow, and very pathetic; but it was varied here and there by a few passages of rapid chanting between the prose. At the end the speaker called on all the people to pray; and first, as they sat, they all stretched out both hands

PERSIAN BRASS-WORKER.

and held them uplifted, with their gaze fixed far away above, as they called "Allah! Allah!" Then all rose up, turned to the east, and murmured a short prayer; the sheikh descended, and the ceremony of the Lailet Ashûra was over.

As one thought on the scene afterwards, it recalled in a new light many classical ideas. One could now see a freshness of meaning in withered phrases like "plangere pectora palmis," "duplices tendens ad sidera palmas," κλαίων δ' ἀμφίσταθ' ὅμιλος, χερσὶ δὲ πᾶσαι στήθεα πεπλήγοντο, Διὶ χεῖρας ἀνασχὼν εὔχετο. One could think of heroes weeping, and feel no laughter at the thought; and one seemed in a measure to understand better the whole cultus of grief with its perennial dirges, like the song of Linus and Ialemus, the mourning for the death of Adonis, Hippolytus, or Narcissus.

But the suggestions of the scene carried one far beyond mere classic memories. Both flagellation and self-mutilation figured in the ancient sun-worship of Persia, and both practices were relics of a time when the shades of the dead were propitiated by human sacrifice. This human sacrifice survived in Mexico at the time of the Spanish conquest; while in the West even as early as Homer we read of the spirits from Hades feasting on the blood of slain animals. It is easy thus to see how the association of bloodshed with mourning arose. Nor is it fanciful to trace something of the same tradition in the monkish flagellants of the Middle Ages: in the warrior Huns savagely wounding themselves round the bier of Attila:* or in the prophets of Baal cutting themselves with knives by the altar on Mount Carmel.

Next morning I went out of curiosity to see Habib, the Persian worker in brass in the bazaars. He said that the men who mutilate themselves take a bath next morning and are none the worse; and he showed me the wounds on his son's head, which certainly were not serious. But it was the men, not the boys or children, who cut themselves in earnest. Habib would have it that no man ever falls out of the procession or faints in the street; but he at once owned that were the wounds inflicted in cold blood, and not under religious excitement, they would often prove mortal. Like the dervishes of the Dôsah, he seemed to believe in a standing miracle.

In the evening at Ismailia Palace the chief of the native jewellers came to the ante-room with some

---

* See Hodgkin's "Italy and her Invaders," vol. ii. p. 192.

marvellous diamonds and precious stones. A fine opal caused great astonishment to Mustapha.

"What is this?" he exclaimed; "why, there is a fire inside! O Protector!"

"Very like a fire," said 'Ali.

"Now by God the Illustrious, it *is* a fire; only a fool's tongue could deny it."

When summoned to the Khedive with Turâbi, I gave him a long account of the Persian ceremony. Turâbi tried to make light of it saying, "It was a stupid thing not worth the seeing." The Khedive however agreed that it was barbarous and horrible, but not stupid, and wished he could have been present. I then turned the conversation on to the Dôsah, asking if there was any prospect of its being suppressed in the coming year. The Khedive replied that he quite hoped so, that he had many assurances that its suppression would be well received. I compared the Lailet Ashûra and the Dôsah, and gave reasons for thinking the latter the more inhuman of the two. While I again related the horrors I had seen at the Dôsah, the Khedive leaned forward in his chair listening intently. He could scarcely credit my account. He said that he had employed fourteen emissaries at the time to make inquiries about the wounded; but no doctors, native or foreign, knew anything about them: they were all smuggled away by the dervishes. However the Khedive evidently had the matter at heart, and my hopes of seeing the Dôsah abolished rose higher.

Another subject of conversation about this time was the deplorable condition of the mediaeval or "Arab" monuments. The Khedive admitted that decay and wilful destruction were causing many of them to fall in ruins, but hoped, as soon as the Ministry of Public Works should be relieved of pressure, to settle measures for their preservation.* In speaking of the almost countless mosques of Cairo, the Khedive showed a surprising knowledge of their situation and points of interest, and he told me the following legends, which are fully believed by the Arabs.

In the great mosque called El Azhar, which is the centre and university of Arab learning, a vast pillar of light is visible at night reaching from the earth to the heavens, and round the fountain in the courtyard may be seen the spirits of holy men who come down to make ablution. In another part of the mosque, among the forest of columns, a man whose heart is

* A commission has since been appointed, with excellent results.

pure may behold little children in the form of elves or fairies, playing about in the dusk, laughing, running, and making all kinds of wild antics. These little ghosts are said to live in the large boxes which stand round the walls and which belong to students.

Another story is, that near the Bâb Tûlûn every night a solemn council or assembly is holden by the great spirits of the Prophet's family. A certain princess of old is queen and arbitress among the grave and reverend elders; she demands news of them, receives their reports, and asks their opinion. They report, for instance, that such and such a Mudir is a bad man, an evil governor, extortionate and oppressive. Proof is given of his misdeeds, the opinion of the council is taken, and a formal decree pronounced and ratified by the queen. A few days later the Khedive, as actual ruler of Egypt, receives an instinct or inspiration directing him to carry out the decree. As he told this story with his usual animation of manner, Effendina laughed heartily.

The Arabs also thought at this time that the sheikh of the little mosque to the north of 'Abdîn Palace appeared every night sitting on his tomb; he did not like the removal of his sanctuary. They believe also in a famous hero-saint called El Bedâwi, who is seen in various parts of the world, as he travels through the air at will. He generally appears mounted on a fine charger in wartime, fighting for the faithful in the thick of battle. Many soldiers who were in the Russo-Turkish War declare unhesitatingly that they saw him hewing down the infidels. El Bedâwi is obviously the counterpart of the Coptic St. George, just as the latter no doubt has classical ancestors.

CHAPTER X.

Wild flowers at Ramleh—The Dôsah to be abolished—The Khedive's intentions about the slave-trade—Difficulties and opposition—Daûd Pasha and the brigands—Treasure-trove—The golden lions—Turkish comedy—A princess's wedding.

A SHORT visit to Ramleh for Christmas enabled me to see what a transformation the winter had made there. In the summer there was nothing but barren sand, nourishing only the ice-plant; now the sand was furrowed and sprouting with corn. The Beduins farm it in the winter months and gather a scanty crop of grain. Wild flowers also had quite changed the face of the country—flowers that stern summer kills and kindly winter brings to life. Among them was a crocus with white and purple blossoms thriving in the most hopeless-looking desert soil, and a very pretty flower, something like heather, with a long ruby-coloured bell-shaped blossom, and many other varieties unknown in England. The sand thus set with bright-hued blossoms shone like enamelled gold.

Before I went I had the great satisfaction of hearing from the Khedive that the Dôsah was henceforth abolished. I could not help showing great gladness at the news and saying how much the Khedive's action would be praised and honoured, especially in England; and I mentioned that last spring I had seen in *The Times* an article which commented on the presence of the Viceroy at the ceremony.

"Well," he said, "I will tell you with frankness: there were two reasons why I could do nothing last spring. For one thing, the old fanatic Sheikh el Bekri was head of the dervishes; for another, it was too soon after my accession for so violent a measure. People did not know me well enough, and it would have been impolitic to begin at once with a reform so sweeping; it would have startled them and made them suspicious. After all I have not been on the throne two years, and I think I have done pretty well."

About a fortnight later, during some small-talk, the Khedive exclaimed suddenly, "By-the-way, a curious coincidence has happened. You know that I have determined to abolish the Dôsah this year, and that the Sheikh el Bekri died not long ago;

well, now the news is, that the sheikh who for many years has ridden the horse over the bodies has just breathed his last. It is singular, very singular."

"It is the removal of your greatest difficulty."

"And there is another curious thing: the horse used for the Dôsah is very ill. So all the people are saying, 'The Khedive wished to abolish the Dôsah, and what's this? Why, first the Sheikh el Bekri died, now the Sheikh of the Horse is dead, and the horse is very ill and—who knows?—will die to-morrow! What can this mean? Surely God is with the Khedive and prospers him.'"

"Doubtless the people speak the truth," I said.

"Well," he continued, "when I first had the idea, I consulted all the 'Ulema, and found them very shy and reserved on the subject. They allowed that the Dôsah was against our religion, but were afraid of the people. I sent for the Sheikh el Islâm, told him my views, and demanded his opinion. He looked very grave indeed, and remained solemn and silent, giving no answer. I argued with him for nearly two hours to prove that it would be a right and a popular measure; but he refused to speak out his mind. At last I said to him, 'I see what the state of things is. You are afraid of the people, and I am not. You think you cannot do it, and I think I can. What is more, I mean to do it. The Dôsah is abolished by order of the Khedive.' When I spoke thus, the Sheikh el Islâm's manner changed, and his face brightened. 'Ah, if Your Highness orders it,' he said, 'that is another thing altogether; the people will be delighted to obey, if they know that it is the order of the Khedive.'

"I am the only person in Egypt who could have done this. All the sheikhs together, all the ministers, all the European consuls, could not have done it. I have succeeded because the people know that I am a good Musulman and that I have my religion at heart; and they believe in me now that I have declared the Dôsah contrary to religion. The ceremony is a base corruption; it was not ordained by Mohammed. Indeed the Korân says that the greatest respect is due to the human person; and how does such a ceremony consist with a respect for humanity? I have also ordered the eating of glass and serpents, cutting with knives, and other barbarous practices, to be abolished. As for the dancing and howling dervishes, they do no harm; their customs are foolish, but innocent, and may be left to die out naturally with the advance of education. In changing the Dôsah too I thought it better to change the scene, and to remove the celebration of the Prophet's birthday to another locality. It will no longer be at Bulâk, but in the 'Abbasiah desert. Riaz Pasha feared this would be too revolutionary; but I determined to have it done. It is better on sanitary grounds; it is better for the people of the Bulâk quarter; and it will help to break up the old associations. Then I mean to give the people plenty of fireworks and salutes of cannon from the citadel to amuse them."

This recital filled me no less with thankfulness than with admiration for the Khedive's splendid courage. I told him my feelings in words that need not be recorded. He then changed the subject and said,

"I am now in the midst of a great matter, a very great matter. I wish to make a decree for the total abolition of slavery in all my territories. By the convention with the English Government the selling of slaves from house to house is allowed till 1884; I want however to declare all slaves free by decree forthwith. I meet with great opposition from my ministers, Riaz Pasha and others. They say, 'It will be impossible; there will be endless difficulty about wills and inheritances. Thus a slave freed by decree will go to the British consul and claim a share in a legacy left by a master to such slaves as he has voluntarily enfranchised.' But I said to Riaz, 'I do not understand you. If a freed slave claims property in this manner, produce the will. You find the clause, *I bequeath to my slave whom I have liberated such and such things*. Ask the claimant how he procured his freedom; and if he says *from the decree*, confront him with the will, and send him about his business; but if he says *from my master's act*, make him produce his liberation papers. What do you say to that, Riaz Pasha?' The Prime Minister was quite dumb; he could not answer a word for some time; then he returned to vague objections that the British consul would always be making difficulties."

I said, "That is obviously ridiculous. Your Highness knows very well that not merely the British consul, but all England and all Europe would applaud such a decree. There is nothing you could do more certain to win sympathy and confidence in England; it would be the crowning proof of your desire to further civilization in Egypt. No doubt there would be some difficulties of detail at first; no great reform can be made without shocking some prejudices and damaging some interests. But such disarrangements would soon be righted, and your decree would triumph. I fear that your ministers and nobles are not so enlightened as yourself in these matters; they suggest difficulties because they desire them. In their hearts they love slavery, and would be very sorry to see it abolished. I feel convinced that it is only a question of courage. When the abolition of the Dôsah was first mooted, these people made long faces and prophesied all manner of evil. And now, although they have motives of self-interest as well, their chief idea is fear of responsibility, which is part of the native character. Your Highness has not this fear; and, if you act with courage, you will succeed in this case as you have succeeded in the other."

"I hope so, and I believe you are right," replied the Khedive; "but Riaz also told me that slavery was an institution of our religion, sanctioned and enjoined by the Korân. This made me very angry, and I answered, 'I think I know our religion better than you, and perhaps better than any one else in Egypt. The Korân, in sanctioning slavery, merely declares that it is lawful to keep as slaves prisoners taken in war; it does not know of or sanction any thing like a traffic in slaves.'"

"Yes," I said, "and I think the Korân also declares that if a slave has served well and desires his freedom, the master shall grant it, and shall give him money likewise. Moreover, the Korân declares, as you were remarking just now, that the greatest respect is due to the person of a man. How is respect for humanity shown by those who buy and sell human beings like so many oxen or camels? No doubt slavery is contrary to the Mohammedan religion."

"That is the truth," answered the Khedive. "Well, I am very busy upon the matter. Every day I am giving two or three hours to it, thinking and conferring. I told Riaz Pasha that I should be willing to call a council of 'Ulema and to consult them. They will all be opposed to the change; but when they understand that I have determined it they will no doubt give way, and even perhaps help me cordially. They are convinced at heart that I am incapable of acting against our religion. Count Sala tells me that there are cases of slaves being bought by pashas in Cairo now; I say that he must find them out, report their names, and have them punished. But in a few months I hope the decree will be issued, and then slavery will be over."

Here Turâbi Bey, who was the only other person present, and whose deafness prevented him from hearing very well, put in a remark:

"Yes, yes; slavery will be over some day, but it will take a very long time: years—perhaps centuries. It cannot be abolished now; that is impossible."

I turned on him and said, "Why do you say that, Turâbi Bey? It is not true. If only His Highness will act of his own will and authority, slavery can and will be abolished at once. If it is left alone, it may take centuries, but the Khedive can put it down now." Then, addressing the Khedive, I added, "Your Highness will, I hope, have the credit of the result. I am sure that Riaz Pasha does not desire the abolition of slavery. People in England believe in him, and are too ready to fancy that all good comes from his initiative. No doubt if slavery ceases, he will look for applause."

Turâbi said very justly, "That is the policy of Riaz; he tries to get the reins of power into his own hand, and he likes to pose as a champion of reform for Egypt."

"Yes," said the Khedive, "I had to tell him the other day, when he questioned a decoration I had given, that it was not his business: that I was sovereign of Egypt: that I could dismiss him at pleasure: and that he might remember the fact."

"Whatever Your Highness may think," I replied, "the Arabs, I believe, look not to him but to the Khedive."

"That is quite true. It is my aim to be loved in the hearts of my people, as I have always striven to gain the goodwill of those about me in private life. I have no ill pride, and nothing pleases me more than making other people happy. It was the same before I came to the throne. In those times all my household were well treated; if a man was ill I went to see him in his room, if he was in trouble I sympathised with him; and every one was paid every month, even in those times when all public salaries were long in arrear. Only once was there any difficulty, and then I sent for a French merchant and sold him all my ostriches."

More political talk followed, but what I have related shows how enlightened and full of promise were the Khedive's own ideas. I subsequently learned that the most serious check to the Khedive's advance in the slavery question was presented by the Mohammedan law, which declares that a slave has no testamentary power; his goods must revert to his master at death. It is obviously the interest of the ruling classes to maintain this arrangement, and the hopelessness of separating the tangle of Mohammedan law and Mohammedan religion gives them every advantage. The people would say that the decree was against the faith, and would treat it as a dead letter. The Khedive therefore appealed earnestly to the Sheikh el Islâm to issue a "fetwah," or official interpretation, explaining away the textual difficulty; but the sheikh resisted with vicious obstinacy.

The next evening the conversation turned on the security of life and property in Egypt compared with the violence of fifty years ago. The Khedive told a story of a certain Latîf Bey, who, in the time of Mohammed 'Ali, went to Stambûl, and, by means of intrigue, got a firmân appointing him governor-general of Egypt. Armed with this he returned. Mohammed 'Ali was away from Cairo; Latif therefore went to the vizier, who welcomed him with smiles and congratulations. The pasha said he would arrange everything for the proclamation and procession on the morrow. Next day Latif Bey appeared at the time appointed, and was received with every honour. On departing he went down to the foot of the staircase and was about to mount his horse, when the vizier suddenly exclaimed, "I have sworn to my friend and sovereign Mohammed 'Ali never to betray him, but to serve him to the death, and do you think I will desert him for a dog like you?" Ere Latif could recover from his surprise, at a sign from the pasha, a kawass lifted his sword and with one blow smote off the usurper's head. The vizier sent it in a basket by an express dromedary to Mohammed 'Ali in Upper Egypt.

The Khedive also said it is quite true, as reported, that Tufida Hânim, daughter of Mohammed 'Ali, used to decoy handsome men into her palace, whence they never returned alive. Her eunuchs used to set upon them and kill them. But a certain Frenchman, so entrapped, took pistols, and when the eunuchs attacked him he shot the foremost. As the others hesitated, he ran, and climbed a tree from which he escaped over the wall.

Yet, though life is now tolerably secure, certain remote districts are from time to time infested with bandits. Previous to the governorship of Daûd

Pasha at Kaineh in Upper Egypt, about ten years ago, there were so many robbers and cut-throats about that no one dare go alone into the fields by day or the streets by night. But Daûd Pasha soon stamped out the plague. All prisoners charged with crimes of violence were thrown into a jail which contained a deep pit or dungeon. In the dungeon dwelt a large and deadly snake, which quickly killed a criminal. Time after time, as it was reported that a prisoner had been killed by a snake, Daûd Pasha feigned an ever-fresh astonishment. But he was fond of such surprises; and the convenient serpent saved all trouble of trial or proof, imprisonment or execution. It was a cruel device, and possibly some innocent persons suffered; but Kaineh became as safe as Cairo.

These provincial governors or mudirs have great power. I was shocked at this time to hear that Amîn Bey Esh-shamsi, who had entertained us so handsomely at Zagazig, had just been sentenced to fifteen years' imprisonment on a trumped-up charge of conspiracy. The fact was that he had quarrelled about a piece of land with the mudir, who was Riaz Pasha's cousin. The same mudir was guilty of an act of the grossest cruelty with the kûrbash, a thong of cowhide which is used to belabour the bare feet of those who cannot or will not pay their taxes. Nominally it had been abolished by Riaz Pasha, who got the credit of the act in a despatch sent by Mr. Malet to the British Government; in fact it remained in use. But the case was hushed up, as diplomacy wished to keep things quiet. So, when the story was reported, diplomacy sent to Riaz Pasha, asking if it were true. Riaz promptly telegraphed to Zagazig, where the mudîr made every arrangement to defeat inquiry. When four days later the official agent arrived, he found the beaten Arabs ready to swear that the mudîr was the tenderest of human beings. But, by dint of cross-examining and questioning other people, he proved that five or six poor fellows had been most savagely beaten, and that one of them had already died from his injuries; he also discovered the place where the kûrbashes used were hidden away. He came back with his facts, but was told, "We cannot take an Arab's evidence; a European's evidence is required,"—as if the mudîr would ask a European to look on at such amusements,—"and then you know we cannot make a disturbance just now; it is not diplomacy."

Yet another story of the mudîr of Zagazig I give as I heard it, without vouching for its truth. Two little boys playing about the rubbish-mounds by the town struck an earthen pot, which proved to be full of treasure. The bulk of the treasure was gold,—necklets, bracelets, rings, and other ornaments of great value: but there were also a score or two of large pearls and some uncut rubies, of such a price that one was sold afterwards for 100*l.* by a Greek, who chanced to buy it as a pretty pebble for a piastre. The news soon travelled to the ears of the mudir, who at once seized and imprisoned the little boys, captured all their remaining treasure-trove, and flogged them unmercifully to make them confess where the rest was hidden. When I heard the story, the boys had been two months in prison, and were kûrbashed periodically to forward their confession. The mudir meanwhile had disgorged most of his spoil to the Government. Thus it is related in the histories, as an Arab would say; he would add, "but God is all-knowing."

One evening I asked the Khedive what was the law about treasure-trove, whether it belonged to the Government, and whether any reward was given to the finder? He said that anything discovered on Government property, which includes waste land, rubbish-heaps, &c., was claimed by the Government, and no reward was given. This I thought bad policy, because the peasants in that case would hide their treasures and sell them to Greeks or travellers; whereas, if even a small reward were offered, they would have some inducement to give them up honestly. The Khedive said that was true, but concealment was very difficult. A peasant seldom worked alone, and if he found any treasure others would see it and give information; or, if not, his wife would gossip. I replied that surely he might find some small object, of the greatest rarity and value perhaps, which he could slip unseen into the folds of his dress, and sell to a passing Greek; and I instanced a most beautiful and unique gold coin of Keos just brought by a traveller. The Khedive replied: "To show you how stringent the law has been, one need not go far; on land held by my own step-mother two magnificent lions of solid gold were found, each eighteen inches long. They had to be given up to the mint, and there they were melted down and coined into four thousand Egyptian guineas."

"Mâ shâ 'llah! What a terrible pity," I said; "it makes one heart-sick to hear of it. Even if money was the one thing needed, why did they not sell the lions?"

"Yes, indeed, it was a sad pity," was the reply.

"Had they been sold they would have brought in 10,000*l.* or 12,000*l.* There was never anything discovered like those lions."

Whether they were sphinxes or veritable lions, which, like those about the throne of Solomon, had adorned some palace of the Pharaohs, I could not ascertain: but it was a most melancholy story.

Few natives, however, except the Khedive, would trouble their heads about such a matter. A curious instance of native indifference arose two or three nights afterwards. Contrary to custom, two pashas were present with the Khedive; but as neither of them understood a syllable of English or French, they did not profit much by the conversation. However, the Khedive happened to appeal to them in Arabic on a point of native usage—the distinction between the black-turbaned Copts and the black-turbaned Muslims. The latter, said the Khedive, wear two little black tassels showing from under the turban, and asked one of the pashas if this was not correct. The pasha answered that the Copts wear a black turban, the Muslims a green one!

"Surely," I said, "the green one denotes a descendant of the Prophet?"

"Of course it does," said the Khedive. "I never

knew anything like these people; they pass all their life here eating, and sleeping, and smoking, and never open their eyes or know one jot of the customs of the country they live in. They have no observation, no memory, no interest. I could not live like that. I am always observing, and I never forget." This is true; the Khedive's memory is extraordinary.

He went on to tell me that great difficulty was being made about the proposed abolition of slavery. Of the four principal sects in Egypt three declared absolutely against the proposal; only the Hanafi approved it. The chief judge of Egypt had been speaking about the suppression of the Dôsah, and said: "I quite approve the idea of putting down barbarous customs contrary to our religion, but I venture to think Your Highness is going too fast, too fast. You wish to make a clean sweep of everything. In the course of some years, gradually, you can abolish first one thing and then another, but not all abuses at a stroke. One should go slowly, not rush at full speed."

Then I inquired whether the Khedive would not suppress the Persian ceremony; to which he replied that it would be very difficult, as the Persians were not natives or subjects, and were, besides, very fanatical.

"But," I said, "at least it would be easy to prohibit the procession in the streets; and to say to these people: 'I dislike your barbarous rites; and, if you do not choose to stop them, at least you shall not parade them in the public streets of my capital.'"

"Yes; it is quite possible to make them conduct the ceremony in private; and in time I hope to reason with the leading Persians, and to talk them over. Then I will scatter a few decorations among them—decorations turn the head," he added, with a good laugh. "So I do not despair of stopping the Lailet Ashûra."

A brief description has already been given of an Arab play; I had now a chance of seeing a Turkish drama. On the first evening of the *fêtes* held to celebrate the marriage of Princess Jamîlah Hânim, an orderly summoned me to the Khedive's presence at the palace of Prince Mahmûd. The prince reproached me with never coming to see him, as I went to see my other friends; and I excused myself, knowing something of oriental compliments. When the Khedive entered, he said: "I want you to see the Turkish play I told you about."

About a dozen courtiers were present in the saloon; we sat on divans smoking. Two musicians were the first to enter, one with a sort of flute, the other with a pair of bowl-shaped drums. They bent to earth in a profound salâm before the Khedive, then retired to a corner, where soon the pipe squeaked most unmusically, the tom-toms rattled, and the play began. It was a sort of comedy, with more talk than action. The first scene showed the hiring of a house by a young wife. She was dressed all in blue silk; an old crone all in crimson, and a maid all in yellow, attended her. The house was represented by a sort of clothes-horse, behind which the women withdrew, of course remaining visible: it was not unlike Snout's wall in Pyramus and Thisbe. As soon as the rent was agreed upon, the husband entered, drunk and incapable, staggering under a large empty basket, which was meant for the family luggage. When he left again, a terrible-looking Jew advanced, accompanied by a bearded dwarf barely two feet high. The Jew was a creditor come to demand payment; and a wrangle which ensued ended in a *mêlée*, during which the dwarf flew about the room on all-fours, attacking the ladies with the speed and agility of a cat. In the midst of the fight entered the drunken husband; the Jew and the dwarf were bundled into the basket, and the husband pulled them about complaining of the weight of the luggage. Two similar scenes followed with a Turkish and Persian creditor, and closed in the same manner; but in the end the husband was confronted by a line of creditors, and his wife avowed her extravagance. This sobered him; he promised payment somewhat tamely, and the comedy ended somewhat lamely.

On the second day of the *fêtes* there was a grand procession, escorting the bride down to Gezirah Palace. A dove was tied by the feet on the top of the bride's carriage to avert the evil eye. In the evening the long avenue of acacias beside the Nile was lighted with lamps; and, as one stood on the bridge, the effect of this line of light ending in a blaze at the palace was very fine. All comers were welcome, and the avenue was thronged with people; soldiers and police, great sheikhs on white asses, turbaned merchants, and smug effendis. Outside the palace gates was a tangle of carriages, turning, pushing, and colliding, as the drivers cursed each other's fathers with savage emphasis.

It was down this avenue that Naib es Sultânah

drove in company with his bosom friend the Mufettish when taking him away to be murdered.

In the gardens of the palace one might see splendid marble fountains upheld by sculptured lions, walks paved with beautiful mosaic, fine statues, and gorgeous kiosks; there were also giant bamboos growing, many curious palms, orange, lemon, and pomegranate trees, poinsettia, magnolia, hibiscus, and other flowering shrubs; and little lakes and streams gave an air of coolness to the scene. The palace itself was ablaze with illuminations; and bands and banquets lasted far into the night.

CHAPTER XI.

Mutiny of the three colonels—Decision of the cabinet council—Conversation with the Khedive—Making an earthquake—Visit of a Persian grandee—His reflections on Egypt—The Prophet's birthday—The Dôsah actually abolished—Conclusion.

ALMOST coincident with these festivities events were happening which proved the beginning of disaster for Egypt, and cost England literally thousands of wasted lives and millions of wasted money.

It was on the 1st February, 1881, that I saw from my windows at 'Abdîn a scene of strange disturbance in the great square before the palace. Bugles were calling, soldiers turning out under arms and rushing about excitedly, orderlies flying at a gallop in every direction. What had occurred is well known. The three colonels, 'Ali Fehmi (whom I well knew, as he was attached to the palace), 'Abdu'l 'Al, and 'Arâbi, having sent an insolent letter to the Minister of War, Osman Pasha, were arrested, and taken to Kasr-en-Nil barracks. While a court-martial was sitting, a band of mutineers burst into the room, attacked Osman Pasha, who escaped through a window, wounded Afflatûn* Pasha, the Under-Secretary, and brought the three colonels back in triumph to 'Abdîn. As they were rushing down to Kasr-en-Nil, the Khedive sent an orderly commanding them to return; they sent back an insolent refusal. Prince Mahmûd met them in his carriage, and sent his aide-de-camp to inquire what they were doing; they replied that the Prince might get down from his carriage and see, if he wanted to know.

Carriages at once came rolling up to the ceremonies, and all the Ministers assembled in council with the Khedive. They debated all day long, and then came to the unfortunate conclusion to pardon the mutineers, to dismiss Osman Pasha, and to make Mahmûd Pasha Sâmi Minister of War, as required by

* Afflatûn is the form in which the Turks, singularly enough, retain the classical "Plato." It may be noted that the Greek ω seems always rendered in Arabic by û (i. e. English oo, as in " boon "), thus kanûn, a musical instrument, is the Greek κανών; ta'ûs is ταώς peacock; arabûn, ἀρραβών, earnest-money. It is possible, however, that the two latter words were borrowed by the Greeks.

the rebels. The Khedive was very uneasy about it all. We told him that in Europe the rebels would have been shot first and heard afterwards; but the council was against strong measures.

Owing to the marriage *fêtes*, it was not till three days afterwards that I had the opportunity of speaking to the Khedive in private on the subject; but, once alone, he began to talk of the mutiny, and spoke of nothing else for three and a-half hours—till midnight. He said his heart was quite heavy, that he could neither eat nor sleep, that he could think of nothing else. He was specially angry that the regiment to which he had shown special favour should have proved so ungrateful. I said it was indeed serious, as he could never feel any confidence in the troops again, but most serious of all because the mutineers had carried their point; they could say: "We acted by violence, and we succeeded." The precedent seemed most dangerous.

"That is true unhappily. Some advise that the mutinous regiments should be let alone for a while, then quietly sent away or punished. What do you think of that?"

"I think that is bad advice, Your Highness; it would not be just or wise to give them the idea that they are pardoned, and then in a month or two to punish them. That would not be punishment but revenge."

"Then what would you do?"

"I would send them away at once, if they are to go at all."

"But the officers have been formally pardoned by decree. When I received 'Ali Fehmi, he kissed my boots not once but a dozen times."

"If they have been pardoned, that alters the case. It is now too late to punish. The sovereign's word is sacred and should be kept sacred."

"You are right, and that is what I told Mr. Malet. I said to him, 'I have pledged my word to pardon them, and it shall and must now be done.' But it is an unfortunate business. I fear we were guilty of great weakness."

"Yes, if I am to speak frankly, it was great weakness. I would never have parleyed with the rebels a moment. First they should have been shot down mercilessly; to suppress the revolt was the first thing; then, when order had been established again, they might have made known their grievance in a lawful manner. At present they have triumphed. Once let these soldiers get the idea that they have only to flourish their bayonets to obtain whatever they choose to demand, then the reign of law is over and government is impossible. They will know that the sovereign power is no longer in the Khedive but in the army."

"Yes, perhaps it was an act of weakness to pardon them. But I do not know. What other course was open? The council of ministers, without one single exception, were for pardon. I called eighteen generals and officers and said to them, 'Can you suppress this mutiny and arrest or disarm or shoot the mutineers?' They all replied 'No, it is impossible. All the troops are wild with excitement, and those under our orders are Arabs, like the mutineers, and would not act against them.' It was not only the native officers, but the European, like Stone Pasha and Ploetz Pasha, who said the same thing, and counselled moderation. I do not understand it."

"Nor do I; because the whole army was not disaffected, and in a mutiny there are generally two parties. Had a prompt appeal been made to the loyalty of the other battalions, I feel sure that a force could have been found to carry out orders."

"Possibly; but the fact is that officers and

ministers were thoroughly frightened. I thought for a while of dismissing the whole Cabinet and naming a new one to shoot the mutineers. But I knew very well that Europe would have said that I had managed the whole affair to get rid of Riaz; just as my father two years ago arranged the military demonstration which enabled him to overthrow Nubar Pasha's ministry. I told this to Mr. Malet, and said, 'Had I acted thus, you would have been the first to accuse me of such double-dealing.' He made no answer. In the same way the German consul-general said to me, 'If Your Highness intends to dismiss the Cabinet, I beg to submit that my Government formally opposes that measure.' I replied, 'I have no such intention, and your Government need not trouble itself to oppose anything.' But you see the difficulties?"

"Yes, indeed," I replied, and the conversation then took a turn which I do not feel at liberty here to follow. But a course of action was arranged for the morrow in a manner that proved satisfactory. When all was settled, the Khedive recurred to the main point and said he feared the Government had shown great weakness. Once more I admitted the fact, and said that at all risk there should have been some effort to make an example of the mutineers on the spot. A handful of resolute men might have done it. The Khedive assented, but added, "I think Riaz greatly to blame. He had warning twenty days beforehand, and neither informed me nor took any measure of precaution." This was astonishing. I told the Khedive that I thought he had been very badly advised all through, and insisted on the need of great firmness should another such trouble arise.

"Have no fear for that," said the Khedive. "It has been a most unhappy business, but at least it has served me as a lesson. They shall know who is sovereign, and what my power is, if ever they revolt again."

From time to time, after the above conversation, the Khedive discussed the state of affairs, and kept me informed of what was passing in his mind and with the army. One day he recounted a dialogue which he overheard between two soldiers working under the palace window. They blamed their officers a good deal; and one remarked, "Effendina has always been very good and kind to us; and remember, he is a very great person. He loves God, and God is with him, and all the prophets are with him, and all the sheikhs, and all the people. **Why, my** friend, that man, if he likes, by the word of his mouth can make an earthquake!"

Talking of the ignorance of the people the **Khe**dive said that the word for an Egyptian in Turkish is "craven but shameless." The Egyptians have no head, no public spirit. If ever they attempt to follow politics, they get hold of the most ridiculous ideas; thus their last idea is that Riaz is trying to sell Egypt to the English for money.

About a fortnight after the mutiny, the Khedive received a visit from a Persian grandee, Hissâm el Sultânah, uncle of the Shah. He was then an old man, variously reported to be seventy or eighty years of age, but had just completed his pilgrimage to Mecca, and had come to Egypt on his way returning. A large retinue accompanied him—a retinue which proved that not even his grey hairs had delivered him from the canker of that vice which is corroding the very heart of Persia.

In Alexandria, as one by one the palaces of the merchant princes, chiefly Greeks, were pointed out, the Persian exclaimed, "Mâ shâ 'llah! Oh the pity! Poor Egypt!" When he was received by the Khedive in Cairo, he came in robes resplendent with jewels. His fingers were cased with rings, one of which contained a brilliant as large as a shilling; his uniform was ablaze with decorations; his sword-hilt and scabbard flashed with emeralds, rubies, and sapphires; and over all he wore a flowing robe of cashmere with diamond buttons. He was amazed at the plainness of the Khedive's attire and of his sword, which was that of an ordinary pasha, unjewelled.

"Is not Your Highness Khedive of Egypt?" he asked. "Why then have you not a better sword than that? Bismallah!"

"Oh," said the Khedive, "I am not one of those who care about jewels. You see even my studs and sleeve-links are of plain gold," and he showed them to the Persian, as he did to me in relating the story.

"Mâ shâ 'llah! Mâ shâ 'llah! God has enlightened my understanding; but in my country this is not the manner of kings. Their custom is to wear many jewels. We love them even as women."

In the evening the grandee went with the Khedive to the theatre, and looking round the house exclaimed, "And are all these people infidels and Franks?"

"Yes, nearly all."

"Verily this is a thing to be recorded in books. May God compensate Your Highness. Truly my heart is cut in pieces to see the affliction of Egypt. But, in shâ 'llah, when the finances mend, then you will drive them all out of the country?"

"Well," said the Khedive, "the finances will not soon mend so far as that. We have a debt of 60,000,000*l*. and if I see it reduced to 30,000,000*l*. I shall be quite content."

Looking at Rossi, the famous Italian actor, who was the star of the evening, the Shah's uncle said, "Is *that* the great man? Truly his mouth is the mouth of a mechanic!"

Again he questioned, "Do you like the English?"

"Yes, I like them"

"At that I am very much astonished. In Persia we do not like them at all. We are very unhappy; for we are between two great enemies, Russia to the north and England to the south. We are in great fear of both. O Protector!"

But now the time had come round again to celebrate the Prophet's birthday; and, though I could not doubt the Khedive's word, I could scarcely believe the good news that the infamous Dôsah, which I witnessed a year ago, was for ever abolished. The festival lasts several days, and hitherto the Dôsah had been the grand finale. On the first day the Khedive sent an orderly inviting me to come down and see the " fantasia."

It transpired at once that the scene was changed from Bulâk to 'Abbasiah—a strong earnest of the Khedive's promise. An open square about half-a-mile in diameter was marked out by tents in the desert; and the approaches to it were bordered with stalls of sweetmeats. The stall is a sort of counter on which the vendor sits cross-legged in the middle of his wares, holding a pair of scales. The chief delicacies are figures, towers, pulpits, &c., in sugar, and a sweet called " razl-el-banât," or " maiden's tangle," which looks like very fine threads of glass. Here too are seen family groups sitting round a brazier and drinking coffee; men carrying wicker trays of bread, and shouting " Allah, Allah "; water-carriers clinking their cups to the words, " Sweet water, O ye thirsty"; beggars crying aloud, " I am the guest of God and the Prophet," or " I ask of my Lord a cake of bread; with thee, O Lord, is my supper"; and here and there men lying asleep, with muffled heads, unconscious of the noise around them. The amusements were somewhat too European, with the exception of the disgraceful phallic play, which is eminently Egyptian. At this one may see young girls looking on without the least sense of shame, and men holding up tiny children to give them a better view.

The majority of the tents which framed the great square were splendid fabrics belonging to the sheikhs of the various religious orders; and each sheikh had every night and almost all night long a solemn service of prayer performed by his own dervishes. The words of this "zikr" are often nothing but "La Allah ill' Allâh" (there is no God but God); but one hears little more than "Allah," or rather "Ullah," repeated hundreds of times in regular cadence. As a number of men gurgle the word out together from those hoarse depths of the throat which only an Arab and his camel possess, it resembles in a more guttural key the ferocious rumbling growls that form the interspaces in a lion's roaring. These noises are accompanied by a furious bobbing and jerking of the whole frame, up and down, backwards and forwards, faster and faster, till the men's eyes become dazed and their mouths covered with foam, every muscle straining at every movement with a terrific emphasis of assertion and belief. The zikr sometimes lasts for more than two hours: but when it is over the men disperse, laughing and chatting as if nothing had happened: all traces of their frenzy vanish in a moment. One of the sheikhs, on being asked what was the use of the zikr, replied that it cleansed the heart and made it pure.

On the fourth day—which had been the day of the Dôsah last year—I went down in a carriage to see the great procession, which, as usual, was to pass before the tent of the Khedive. About one o'clock, in a storm of driving sand, the great banners of the dervish orders were seen advancing; pipes and cymbals and tomtoms resounded, while with the musicians marched singers chaunting verses of the Korân or the brief and simple creed of the Muslims. Ere long appeared the Sheikh of the Horse, the successor of the man who rode over the bodies last year. He was mounted on a black Arab barb and robed in cream-coloured silk; he wore a green turban, decked with embroidery, which stood out nearly a foot all round his head. Fifty yards before him marched a strong body of police, obviously meant to prevent any fanatics at the last moment from throwing themselves under the horse to be trampled. But nothing of the kind happened. There was not the faintest attempt or faintest sign of a wish on the part of any dervish to have his bones broken. The Sheikh of the Horse was the only man who suffered, or pretended to suffer: for it seems his business to go through a series of fainting-fits on grand occasions.

When the sheikh had passed, company after company followed, each with its own chief, mounted on horse or donkey as his purse decided. Every chief was preceded by a henchman bearing his prayer-carpet folded, and round about him all his banners waved and all his tomtoms clattered. Face after face I scanned, but saw no sign of unnatural excitement, such as arises from hashish or râki, and above all none of that revolting drunken pallor which last year rendered so many faces hideous. Nor were there any naked men carrying knives and axes; no swordsmen cutting themselves, or spike-bearers thrusting their spikes through cheeks and arms; no eaters of glass or serpents.

As each company reached the end of the line of tents the banners were lowered and folded, the sheikh dismounted, and his followers dispersed.

So passed in perfect order and tranquillity the first festival of the Prophet's birthday without the Dôsah. The impossible was accomplished: and so was abolished a degrading and inhuman custom which for two centuries had been the principal feature in the most solemn of all the Mohammedan festivals of Egypt. No one who thinks what this statement means can refuse to the Khedive the admiration and honour which he deserves for his most noble courage. I, for one, who know how much evil he conquered, shall never cease to revere him for it.

But my time in Cairo was now drawing to a close. For reasons, which I need not here record, I had resolved to return to England. The Khedive's farewell to me was most touching in its heartfelt kindness: and to me it was a real sorrow to part from him and from the little princes. Like all who have ever been in the personal service of the Khedive, I retain for him a feeling of loyal devotion, and I have no patience with the ignorant malice of those in England who slander him.

Nearly all my leisure for months past had been devoted to collecting materials for a work on the ancient churches of the Copts—the living descendants of Pharaoh's Egyptians and the brave upholders of the faith once delivered to them by St. Mark. All the churches near Cairo I learned by heart, and I explored and planned out the lost lines of the great Roman fortress of Babylon at Old Cairo: but it was one of my greatest regrets in leaving that a journey to the desert monasteries by the Natrun Lakes was prohibited by the government, owing to the turbulent condition of the Beduins in that region. But the journey has since been accomplished and the work published.

No one who has lived even a year in Cairo, and has been penetrated with the spirit of Eastern life in that golden city, will ever forget the evening on which he broke with the life for ever, to face again the dreariness of Europe. Yet it was something to have lived it, something to have laid up a great store of uncommonplace memories, something to have seen realised an almost impossible dream of reform. So amid all mournful thoughts of departure there was not wanting the strain of a "*Nunc dimittis.*"

FINIS.

Westminster: Printed by NICHOLS AND SONS, 25, Parliament Street.

www.ingramcontent.com/pod-product-compliance
Lightning Source LLC
Chambersburg PA
CBHW022046230426
43672CB00008B/1086